30 Poems to Memorize
(Before It's Too Late)

30 Poems to Memorize
(Before It's Too Late)

Edited by David Kern

CiRCE Books | Concord, NC

30 Poems to Memorize (Before It's Too Late)
Copyright © 2020 CiRCE Institute
First edition.

Published by:
> The CiRCE Institute
> 81 McCachern Blvd
> Concord, NC 28025

ISBN: 978-1-7347853-1-9

Cover art by Graeme Pitman
Original illustrations by Kirstie Ruffatto

Printed in the United States of America

*Don't you just love poetry that gives you
a crinkly feeling up and down your back?*

—Anne of Green Gables

Contents

PREFACE

IT IS SAID THAT WE LIVE IN THE INFORMATION AGE. We can have any piece of data we want at our fingertips—all it takes is a few taps, maybe a swipe or a scroll. We can know anything, anytime, and for any purpose. And some things we might even remember—at least in bits and pieces. This is both a blessing and a curse. On the one hand, knowledge truly can be powerful. It can free us from fear, enable us to accomplish things we didn't think were possible, or show us how to get from one place to another. It can make us experts in ways previous generations never would have imagined. And yet we all know the inherent limitations of this knowledge. We know that it is incomplete, that it is tethered to tools that are outside our control, that it is not really our own—and thus, that its ability to truly transform us is limited.

For centuries, however, since man first began to pass along his most cherished stories, he relied on what he could remember. He valued a mind capable of being full of things that were not just useful, but also true, good, and beautiful. Memory was not just a tool for individual use but was in fact the collection point for all culture and tradition.

As recently as one hundred years ago, our culture still valued memory as an essential good—as a necessary component of being fully human and truly educated.

Poetry has always been a part of that. Even in an age when every great poem can be ours within a few seconds, mankind must fill its collective mind with great verse—with lines and language and images and forms that nourish the imagination. Of course, poetry lovers have always spoken of the need for learning verse by heart, and many actually do try to learn their favorite stanzas. But poetry remembered is more than fancy language saved for later (which is certainly a value in and of itself); it is also beauty running through us, changing us, and altering our essential state. As Catherine Robson wrote in her book *Heart Beats: Everyday Life and the Memorized Poem*, "[i]f we do not learn by heart, the heart does not feel the rhythms of poetry as echoes or variations of its own insistent beat." To memorize is to inhabit and be inhabited by that which is transcendent. Think of it: to make Shakespeare or Dickinson or Keats or Kenyon a part of you.

As a child, I would memorize sports scores and statistics like it was drinking water (to this day, I find that my memory marks dates by sporting events). I would memorize lines from my favorite movies. I would remember jokes and songs and stories and yes, poems. Usually, the things I best remembered were the things I loved the most—things I wanted to spend time with—and so I learned by osmosis. The collection of poems you hold in your hand is designed with that idea in mind: Together we have chosen poems we love, poems readers have been passing on for years, and poems we think you will (or perhaps already do) love, too—poems that are worth loving and memorizing. Hopefully you will want to spend enough time with these poems to learn them by osmosis—as I did with the history of the Green Bay Packers.

We also recognize that memorizing poetry takes effort and that having a guide can be helpful (and freeing). Each poem in this book is accompanied by an essay designed to help you linger in the poem peacefully, thoughtfully, and carefully. These essays are designed to provide questions more than answers in order to help you spend time with the poems in an enjoyable and worthwhile fashion. Our goal, ultimately, is to help jump-start your study, exploration, and enjoyment of poetry—not be the end-stop. If this volume is your entryway to—or serves to revive your experience with—great poetry, then we'll consider it a success. To that end, it's marked throughout with modest definitions of key terms or forms and references to books in which you can learn more about that term or form. Whether you consider yourself a poetry novice or a poetry expert, I hope you'll relish the deep-dives available beyond the pages of this book.

The poets and poems you find on these pages have been chosen specifically because we believe they have properties that make them memorizable, that make them worth putting to heart, and that make them exciting to learn. As we memorize each poem, we participate in the great tradition that they collectively create and preserve. In our efforts at memorizing them, we, too, are helping to preserve that tradition; we, too, are keeping it alive in a way that our swipes, taps, clicks, or scrolls can never do, however powerful the search engine may be.

—David Kern

Six Tips for Memorizing Poetry

For some readers this book will serve as an anthology of good poems to keep handy—like a coffee table book or a cookbook you turn to from time to time. To others, though—the stout of heart among us—it will be a guide to real work, contemplation, and attention. Memorizing poetry, after all, is not for the faint of heart. Of course, as with any task, there are ways to make the process a bit less overwhelming. Here are a few tips for this particular project to help make the work more do-able. Tally-ho!

§

1. Write the poem out by hand, more than once, if possible. Get your senses involved.

2. Find (or record) a read-aloud version and listen two or three times a day for a few days. Let that poem bounce around your subconscious.

3. Identify markers to latch on to: repetitions, memorable images, captivating phrases. Use them as signposts.

4. Memorize in chunks, like couplets, stanzas, or scenes.

5. Let the poem tell you what it is. Every poem has a form, even the most free ones, and when you pay attention to that form, you give your memory the tools to return to it again and again.

6. Don't rush the process. We all memorize at different paces.

A Simple Guide to Reading Poems
By Sally Thomas

The first time you read a poem, read for the lay of the land. Read more than once. Read aloud at least once. When reading aloud, observe line breaks with a brief pause even when the sentence continues beyond the end of the line. Line breaks are always deliberate, and the pushback that they provide against the forward impulse of the syntax contributes to the tension and sense of urgency that animates a good poem. Never read a poem as if it were prose. Copy the poem out by hand to make your mind "listen" to it slowly and carefully. Have a dictionary on hand, but don't use it until you've read the poem at least once all the way through.

On a subsequent reading, ask yourself the following:
- Are there unfamiliar words?
- Are some familiar words used in an unfamiliar way?
- What multiple meanings might even a familiar word have,

1

and how many of those meanings might be in play as the word is used here?

As you read, consider how the poem looks on the page. Is it an unbroken block of text? Are the stanzas of a regular length? That is, are they two, three, four, or more lines, consistently with white space between stanzas? Are they in irregular stanzas? How many lines are in the poem in all? Are the lines short or long? Are the lines endstopped—that is, is the end of the line the natural end of or a break in the sentence? Are the lines enjambed—that is, do the lines stop but the sentence keeps going, spilling over into the next line or lines, breaking at what may seem like unnatural or awkward places?

Read for patterns of sound. Are there rhymes at the ends of lines? These are called, not unpredictably, end-rhymes. Can you discern a regular pattern of end-rhymes? For example:

Rhyming couplets:

I am His Majesty's Dog at Kew;
Pray, tell me, sir, whose dog are you?

Or quatrains, which might look like this:

That time of year thou mayst in me behold
When yellow leaves, or none, or few, do hang
Upon those boughs which shake against the cold,
Bare ruined choirs, where late the sweet birds sang.

Or this:

When I consider how my light is spent
Ere half my days in this dark world and wide,
And that one talent which is death to hide
Lodged with me useless, though my soul more bent

Are there rhymes within lines, also called internal rhymes? Rhyme often ties words together in interesting ways, generating resonances of meaning from these juxtapositions. Consider what relationships might exist between rhyming words and how thinking about those relationships might enlarge your vision of the poem.

Are there repetitions of words and/or sounds? Do you hear the same consonant sound repeated—what is known as alliteration—either within a line or over a group of lines? Do you hear assonance—the repetition of a particular vowel sound? What effect do these repetitions suggest in your ear or your mind? Sometimes alliteration and assonance can create sound effects, as in the lapping lake water of Yeats' "Lake Isle of Innisfree," but like rhyme, they can also highlight relationships between words.

Can you hear any regular "beat" or rhythm in the poem? Read it aloud again, and clap or tap the stressed syllables as you say them to see whether there is a regular number of stressed syllables per line. How many do you hear?

Read for voice and sense. Who is speaking in the poem? Note that when talking about a poem, we usually do refer to the speaker, rather than the poet, as saying this or that. The voice that speaks in a poem is more like a character in fiction than like the writer's own personal voice—that poetic voice is an artificial construct in the same way and should not be confused with the real-life person of the poet even if there's not a huge divide between the two. Never assume, on the basis of details divulged by a poem's speaker, that you know anything about the poet's private life.

Read for point of view. Is the poem's speaker a first-person speaker ("I")? Is the poem's speaker using the second person, addressing a "you"? Is the poem's speaker a third-person speaker, possibly omniscient, describing the actions or thoughts of a he, a she, or an it? Is there anyone else in the poem, or is the speaker talking to himself or herself? Does the poem refer to external events (this happened, then this happened, and then I did this other thing), or is it more like following the trajectory of someone's thought process or a series of associations with their own kind of logic? Does time move or stand still? To what kind of effect do all these things seem to add up? Do you sense a particular mood in the poem? Can you point to specific words and phrases that contribute to that mood? Do you sense a larger view of the universe operating in the poem—a kind or unkind universe, a universe in which there is God and mercy and grace, or a universe without those things? Hope or despair? Love or bitterness? What words and phrases hint at these things? Whether the poem deals with external events or with internal thoughts and feelings, do you sense why these events or thoughts and feelings are important? What makes them urgent?

Reflect. Having read the poem carefully, what about it seems most important, beautiful, or worth thinking about to you? Consider what identifiable elements in the poem have contributed to the sense you have derived from it. Consider that it's all right if multiple contradictory things seem to be in play at once—beauty and darkness, for example—and that your ultimate experience of a poem may be as emotionally or cognitively layered, complex, and inexplicable as your own lived, human experience. This is, after all, what a poem seeks to do—to render some human experience into illuminating language and to invite you into it.

A Note on Scansion for Novices

Scansion, or the discernment of a poem's meter, is an art deserving its own separate essay. Suffice it to say that, traditionally understood, a line of poetry contains metrical feet, each of which in turn contains a set pattern of stressed and unstressed syllables, as follows:

- *The iamb:* one unstressed and one stressed syllable, like the name Michelle.
- *The trochee:* one stressed and one unstressed syllable, like the name Michael.
- *The anapest:* two unstressed syllables and one stressed syllable, like the phrase, "In a while."
- *The dactyl:* one stressed syllable and two unstressed syllables, like (ironically), the word "anapest."

Meter, in a vastly oversimplified nutshell, is identified in terms of the number of feet in a line and what kind of feet they predominantly are. For example, when you encounter a consistent pattern of five iambs in a line—"My mistress' eyes are nothing like the sun," for example—we identify the meter as iambic (predominantly composed of iambs) pentameter (five to a line).

A Note on Rhyme Scheme for Novices

When we want to talk about rhyme scheme, we assign each end rhyme a letter. The sound ending the first line of a poem is always given the letter A. Any line ending that rhymes with A is also identified as A. The first differing rhyme that occurs, whether it occurs in the next line, the one after that, or wherever, is given the letter B, and so on. So the rhyme scheme of a poem composed entirely of couplets would be AABBCCDD, with each couplet given a new letter.

The following poets have been arranged in alphabetical order, this being the simplest approach. The order is not meant to indicate a hierarchy of poets although such a debate might be worth having. We invite you to take up the cause for your favorite poet via a carefully worded sonnet or ode.

W. H. Auden
1907–1973

Best known for: "The Shield of Achilles,"
"Funeral Blues," "For the Time Being"

Wystan Hugh Auden was an English-born poet, essayist, and professor who won the Pulitzer Prize for Poetry in 1947. His debut book of poetry, *Poems*, emerged thanks in large part to the support of T. S. Eliot, who championed Auden's early work and helped make him a household name. In fact, much like Eliot, Auden's poems are musically complex reflections on the spiritual and intellectual malaise of World-War-era life, poems which hold up remarkably well nearly a century later. He was a political poet with a sense for the literary and a literary poet with a sense for the social. To this day, he remains one of the most influential poets of the era. Indeed, poet Joseph Brodsky once called Auden "the greatest mind of the twentieth century," a bold claim that, while perhaps hyperbolic, certainly speaks to the degree to which Auden's work holds claim on the imagination of his readers.

{poem}
If I Could Tell You

Time will say nothing but I told you so,
Time only knows the price we have to pay;
If I could tell you I would let you know.

If we should weep when clowns put on their show,
If we should stumble when musicians play,
Time will say nothing but I told you so.

There are no fortunes to be told, although,
Because I love you more than I can say,
If I could tell you I would let you know.

The winds must come from somewhere when they blow,
There must be reasons why the leaves decay;
Time will say nothing but I told you so.

Perhaps the roses really want to grow,
The vision seriously intends to stay;
If I could tell you I would let you know.

Suppose all the lions get up and go,
And all the brooks and soldiers run away;
Will Time say nothing but I told you so?
If I could tell you I would let you know.

{reflection}

The Hope of Unknowing
by Emily Andrews

The quiet rhythms of an average day gently deceive us into believing we maintain control over our future. When unlooked-for tragedy strikes, however, it indelicately strips that lie away and exposes our incurable blindness. In such a helpless condition, we find ourselves entirely dependent on forces outside our control. Whether those forces are malevolent, indifferent, or loving is then the question at hand and must inevitably influence the attitude we carry into days ahead. But how can we be sure of the attitude the universe will take toward us?

When English American poet Wystan Hugh Auden published "If I Could Tell You" in 1940, the future must have looked bleak indeed. The Second World War had just begun, and Auden had moved to the United States on a temporary visa. Informed by the British army that his return was unnecessary, he watched helplessly as his homeland crumbled (quite literally) across the sea under the pressure of German bombings. Both Auden's personal life and the future of Western civilization looked highly uncertain.

The poet's haunting reflection on this theme comes to us as a **villanelle**—a form well-suited to memorization, given its frequent repetition. The repeated phrases, or refrains, are found in the first and third lines of a villanelle's opening tercet—a stanza of three lines. In "If I Could Tell You," those phrases are "Time will say nothing but I told you so" and "If I could tell you I would let you know."

It is interesting to note the differing sentiments of these refrains. The first suggests the indifferent, if not hostile, attitude of unrelenting time towards humanity. The second, however, indicates the speaker's active, affectionate feeling for his listener. These two refrains alternate as the last line to each succeeding tercet and then close the poem in a couplet. The effect is to draw out tension between the cold experience of an impersonal Nature and the loving attention found in personal

---

Villanelle {a form worth remembering}

A form that has its roots in Italian folk songs and sixteenth century French verse, it is defined by:

- nineteen lines divded into six stanzas (five tercets, one quatrain)
- The first line of the poem repeats as the third line of the second and fourth stanzas and the third line of the sixth stanza.
- The third line of first stanza repeats are the third line of the third and fifth stanzas and the final line of the poem.
- The repeating lines rhyme, leading to an ABA rhyme scheme.

Learn more in Edward Hirsch's *A Poet's Glossary*, page 683.

relationships between individuals.

The rhyme scheme of a villanelle follows an ABA pattern in the first five tercets and ends with an ABAA scheme in the final quatrain. One aspiring to memorize a villanelle must therefore simply contend with two end rhymes, in this poem words rhyming with "pay" or "know." Even these two words alone portray the central conflict of the piece. Does the world operate on an unfeeling economy of debt and payment, or is the more comforting exchange of knowing and being known reflected in the order of the universe?

The very sounds of the poem continue on this theme. The most repeated of these are "o" and "s." The assonance of varied "o" sounds in words like "nothing," "should," and "show" reverberate hollowly through the lines. They are sounds of woe and suffering. The sibilant "s," however, in words like "say," "because," and "reasons" offer sounds of reassurance. They are the tones a mother would use to hush her child.

One of the most interesting elements of this poem is its rhythm. A villanelle has no strict metrical scheme, although most twentieth-century villanelles follow iambic pentameter. Auden participates in this tradition but in an irregular fashion. It is one of those exciting instances where the poet's use of meter reflects his thematic concerns—an excellent opportunity to introduce students to the idea that a poem's mechanics hold significance.

The first seven lines of this poem have no regular meter. In the opening line, Auden uses two dactyls (a stress with two unstressed syllables) and two iambs (an unstressed syllable followed by a stressed syllable). In the second line, however, he uses a dactyl, a trochee (a stressed syllable followed by an unstressed syllable), a dactyl, and an iamb. It is chaotic—a random sequence of metrical feet that mirrors the speaker's sense of time's uncertainty.

By way of content, these first two tercets express man's helplessness in the face of the silent march of time. Whatever predictions we make about days to come, only the day's arrival will reveal the truth. By saying "I told you so," we also sense the truth will be bleak and contrary to our preferred vision of the future. The happy days of childhood, represented by a clown's entertainment, will produce the contrary effect of weeping as we confront the trials of adulthood. Perhaps Auden, himself a Shakespeare scholar, was thinking here of the Bard's clowns with their serious pronouncements. Furthermore, the poem reminds us that as we come upon our elder years, joyous dance will turn to stumbling. Shakespeare's comedies ended with dancing as well in order to reflect a final harmony in nature. Maybe Auden is suggesting that our ability to experience life's harmony is hampered by the frailty of human nature. Yet in the eighth line, Auden finally introduces a regular line of iambic pentameter: "Because I love you more than I can say." This is the center line of the five tercets, reflecting its central significance to the poem. The poet anchors steady love for his listener amid the rapid change of time.

From this point on, every line except the two refrains appear in iambic pentameter. The simultaneous turn in the poet's tone is also carried through to the end, transforming time's uncertainty from a sense of helpless determinism to a chance for hopeful expectation rooted in personal relationship. As the ever-changing nature of time is embodied in the blowing winds and decaying leaves, the speaker wonders whether that change originates from some fixed source. Surely reversals come from somewhere and for some reason. We know that the leaves' decay fertilizes the coming spring.

Perhaps, the speaker suggests, the good in life is more permanent than we think, the roses and the beatific vision of summer earnestly looking to last. Could our desire for perpetual youth and beauty, seemingly mocked by the progression of time, actually indicate a deeper reality? The speaker ends by supposing a future where the hindrances to our harmony, the predators and aggressors, leave us behind. The brook's perpetual running could actually be a sign that change is on its way out.

Notice also that Auden slightly alters the poem's first refrain in the end. Shifting it from a declarative to an interrogative sentence, he softens the phrase's fatalistic tone and opens the door to hope. By transforming the refrain into a question, the poet leaves room for Time to tell us more than "I told you so." The previous conglomeration of metrical feet in that line is furthermore recrafted as iambic pentameter here, planting order in the face of the question's uncertainty.

The very problem of the poem is its answer. Hope is only possible from a place of unknowing—a place where time has not had its final word. Significantly, the poet's optimism is mediated through care for an individual—our love for particular people reflecting the terms on which the world was created. In this way, Auden offers comfort and solidarity in times of crisis. We are all equally dependent creatures, and our care for one another is an expression of our hope for better days to come.

Wendell Berry
1934–

Best known for: Sabbath Poems,
Jayber Crow, The Unsettling of America

American author activist, and farmer Wendell Berry was born in Henry County, Kentucky, where his family had farmed the land for more than five generations. He studied English at the University of Kentucky and married his wife, Tanya, in 1957. After studying at Stanford University under novelist Wallace Stegner, Berry began his prolific writing career with the publication of his first novella, *Nathan Coulter*, in 1960. His reputation as an essayist expanded in the tumultuous climate of the 1960s as he became known as an advocate for peace ("A Statement Against the War in Vietnam") and stability ("A 50-Year Farm Bill"). In 1965, Berry and his family settled near his birthplace in Henry County, at a farm called Lane's Landing on the banks of the Kentucky River. Berry lives, writes, and farms there to this day. A versatile author, his skill flows easily across multiple genres. He has published more than fifty books—fiction, poetry, and essays—throughout his career, all of them advocating for people to pursue principled lives in harmony with the natural world. A staunch advocate for small-scale farming, environmental care, and humane communities, Berry contends against the increasingly mechanized nature of corporate "agribusiness," which he claims is at the heart of crumbling American economic, moral, and communal life. As a poet, Berry is at his most intimate, giving voice to his abiding love of nature and enduring human connections. His poetry collections like *The Country of Marriage* and *The Broken Ground*, as well as his famous Sabbath poems, contemplate how a simple life, full of both suffering and joy, can resonate with the rhythms of the natural world. As much as any other contemporary author, Berry celebrates and protects the transcendence of ordinary life in an increasingly denuded culture.

{poem}
Early in the year by my friend's gift

"Why seek ye the living among the dead?"

Early in the year by my friend's gift
I saw at Sansepolcro Piero's vision:
The soliders who guard the dead from the living
themselves become as dead men, one
tumbling dazedly backward. Awake, his wounds
bleeding still, his foot upon the tomb, Christ
who bore our life to its most wretched end,
having thrust off like a blanket the heavy lid,
stands. But for his face and countenance
I have found no words: powerful beyond life
and death, seeing beyond sight or light,
beyond all triumph serene. All this Piero saw.
And we who were sleeping, seeking the dead
among the dead, dare to be awake. We who see
see we are forever seen, by sight have been
forever changed. The morning at last
has come. The trees, once bare, are green.

{reflection}
A New Perspective
by Jeffrey Bilbro

In 1979, Wendell Berry began writing poems during Sunday walks in the woods and fields around his Kentucky home. After more than forty years, these "Sabbath poems" make up a substantial collection of more than three hundred of his poems. As a farmer and essayist, Berry is well known for advocating local food and sustainable agriculture, and in these poems—as well as in his rich fiction—he voices an authentic love for his place and the Creator who sustains its lives.

"Early in the year by my friend's gift" stands out from the other poems in his Sabbath series as it is one of the few ekphrastic poems. Ekphrasis comes from a Greek word meaning "to speak out," and it refers to a poetic or other verbal response to a visual artwork. In this case, Berry is responding to Piero della Francesca's fifteenth-century fresco, *the Resurrection*. Berry's encounter with this painting becomes the occasion for a poetic meditation on the enduring power of Christ's resurrection to reorder all of creation.

Piero's fresco adorns a wall of the town hall in Sansepolcro, Italy. The town derives its name, meaning "Holy Sepulcher," from its founding upon relics that a pair of pilgrims brought from Christ's tomb. The painting is worth contemplating at length—look it up and spend time examining it as you memorize Berry's poem. There are several details worth noting: The soldier in brown leaning against the pole held by Christ is likely a self-portrait of Piero. The painting has two vanishing points: the four sleeping soldiers form one composition, and the risen Christ, standing above them, exists in a separate frame of reference. Finally the trees on the left side of the painting are bare while those on the right are in full leaf, indicating the profound transformation wrought by the Resurrection.

In an essay about Piero, Aldous Huxley alludes to this vegetal transformation in his description of a bus trip over a mountain pass on the way to Sansepolcro:

> *"Our omnibus groaned and rattled slowly up a bleak northern slope, among bald rocks, withered grass and still unbudded trees, it crossed the col and suddenly, as though by a miracle, the ground was yellow with innumerable primroses, each flower a little emblem of the sun that had called it into being."*

Huxley famously declared that, judged on moral standards, Piero's fresco is "the greatest picture in the world." Yet while Huxley takes care to distinguish the moral, classical, and humanistic beauty of

Piero's composition from any genuinely religious meaning or beauty, Berry invites his readers to experience the painting in religious terms.

At the outset, Berry frames this experience as a gift: it is through his friend's gift that he was able to visit Sansepolcro, and Piero's painting depicts the Resurrection as the gift at the vital core of life itself. The poem's loose iambic pentameter swells near the end as some lines stretch to include six or even seven feet (see, for example, the heptameter line "among the dead, dare to be awake. We who see"). Then as if to mark the definitive change that has been effected by the Resurrection, the final two lines fall into almost perfect iambic tetrameter: "forever changed. The morning at last/has come. The trees, once bare, are green."

The second sentence's unfurling syntax focuses our attention on the risen Christ standing boldly above the sarcophagus:

> *Awake, his wounds*
> *bleeding still, his foot upon the tomb, Christ*
> *who bore our life to its most wretched end,*
> *having thrust off like a blanket the heavy lid,*
> *stands.*

If you cut out the four parenthetical descriptions, three spare words are left: "Awake … Christ … stands." This simple sentence—an adjective, a subject, and an intransitive verb—distills the Resurrection to its essence. We are thus confronted with the stark reality of the risen body.

The poem then focuses in on Christ's face only to record a Dantean failure of language. As Dante advances through the levels of Paradiso, he repeatedly confesses his inability to translate what he sees into human language. In the final canto, Dante's words utterly fail to describe his vision of the triune God: "What I could see was greater/ than speech can show." Yet even as his speech falters, he finds himself caught up in "the Love the moves the sun and the other stars."

Similarly, Berry moves from his own failure to name the countenance of the risen Christ to the powerful effects felt by those on whom he turns his face: "We who were sleeping, seeking the dead/ among the dead, dare to be awake." One of the effects is that we, like Christ, are now awake; we now participate in his resurrected life. A second result is that the poet has shifted from the first person singular to the first person plural: He no longer speaks as an "I" but as a "we." Being confronted by this face causes the poet to understand himself as a member of the community comprising those who see that they are seen. He has gone from the "I saw" of the poem's second line to the "we are forever seen" of the fifteenth line.

Caught in the gaze of the resurrected Christ, the poetic perspective buckles in a way that parallels the twin vanishing points in Piero's painting. The poet declares that it is "by sight" that we have been "forever changed." But whose sight causes this enduring transformation? Is it the sight by which we see or the sight by which we are seen? Like the painting, Berry's poem shifts from one frame of reference to another: At first, the viewing subject is the agent, but by the end of the poem, the resurrected Christ is the central actor.

In some ways, the poem's shift suggests an iconic perspective. Whereas Piero was working on the cusp of the Italian artistic tradition that developed linear perspective, many earlier depictions of biblical scenes followed the iconic tradition wherein the vanishing point lies in front of the painting's surface rather than behind it. In other words, viewers are invited to imagine themselves as seen by the holy figures in an icon. (Think, for instance, of Andrei Rublev's famous icon Troitsa where the table and chairs make this reversed perspective particularly apparent.) It is precisely this experience of being seen that Berry records at the end of his poem.

Reciting Berry's poem provides us with an opportunity to experience viscerally this perspectival shift that Christ's resurrection brings into being. When we see him standing wide awake above the tomb, we come to know ourselves as those who are profoundly seen. All of creation participates in the redemption inaugurated at this moment when death itself began working backward. And like the trees in Piero's painting, we who were once bare become green.

Emily Dickinson
1830–1886

Best known for: "Hope is the Thing with Feathers,"
"There is no Frigate Like a Book," "I Felt a Funeral, in my Brain."

American poet Emily Dickinson was born in 1830 in Amherst, Massachusetts, to an influential family. Her father was active in state and national politics, serving as a member of Congress. The Dickinson family was extraordinarily close. The two sisters, Emily and Lavinia, lived at home their entire adult lives while their brother, Austin, lived next door with his family. Emily thrived in her studies at the local Amherst Academy as a child where her education was described by biographer Judith Farr as "ambitiously classical for a Victorian girl." As a young lady, she attended Mount Holyoke Female Seminary for one year before moving back to her family home where she remained for the rest of her life. A famous recluse, Emily was an eccentric personality. Early in her life, she became obsessed with the "deepening menace" of death, an anxiety which would become a unifying theme in her poetic canon. She received few visitors and rarely left her room where she studied and wrote in seclusion, but she carried on a rich correspondence with a few close friends. Dickinson wrote over 1,800 poems, but only ten were published while she was alive. Her sister, Lavinia, discovered Emily's prolific cache of writings after her death. Dickinson's posthumously published poetry became profoundly influential in the landscape of American literature. Known for short lines and stanzas broken by frequent dashes, Dickinson's poetic style was wholly unique in structure and form. Her poetry, influenced by the Metaphysical poets and her Calvinist upbringing, contemplates topics such as death, love, loneliness, and memory, and, along with Walt Whitman, she is known as one of the most influential poets in the development of a characteristically American poetic voice.

{poem}
We grow accustomed to the Dark

We grow accustomed to the Dark —
When Light is put away —
As when the Neighbor holds the Lamp
To witness her Good bye —

A Moment — We Uncertain step
For newness of the night —
Then — fit our Vision to the Dark —
And meet the Road — erect —

And so of larger — Darknesses —
Those Evenings of the Brain —
When not a Moon disclose a sign —
Or Star — come out — within —

The Bravest — grope a little —
And sometimes hit a Tree
Directly in the Forehead —
But as they learn to see —

Either the Darkness alters —
Or something in the sight
Adjusts itself to Midnight —
And Life steps almost straight.

{reflection}
Following an Uncertain Path
by Brian Phillips

As Roger Lundin wrote in *An Inviation to the Classics*, "the family and friends who gathered for Emily Dickinson's funeral in Amherst, Massachusetts, on a sunny afternoon in May, 1886, had no idea that the woman they mourned was one of the greatest lyric poets in the English language." Even when the reclusive genius reached out to editor Thomas Wentworth Higginson, she claimed to have no portrait of herself, choosing instead to describe her appearance as, "Small, like the Wren, and my Hair is bold, like the Chestnut Bur – and my eyes, like the Sherry in the Glass, that the Guest leaves – Would this do just as well?" Dickinson rarely left Amherst and, following the completion of her education at Amherst Academy and Mount Holyoke Female Seminar, willingly chose the life of a single woman. For the last two decades of her life, Dickinson almost never left the grounds of her own home. While some of her poetry was in print during her lifetime, it was not until her death that hundreds more poems were discovered and published despite her wish that they be destroyed.

Dickinson's canon, containing almost exclusively short works, is surprisingly complex; her style is unusual. Upon receiving several poems from her, Higginson was struck both by the poet's talent and by her strange syntax and punctuation. Dickinson appears to have been almost morally opposed to normal punctuation, preferring a liberal use of dashes instead, and she capitalized seemingly any word she felt needed it (habits not restricted to her poetry—as seen in the self-description to Higginson above). Additionally, she had a knack for unexpected metaphors and personifications. For example, in "Because I could not stop for Death," Dickinson portrays death as a gentleman who "kindly stopped" for her, immortality as a leisurely carriage ride, and gravesites as houses. Her topics were vast, covering life, nature, love, time, eternity, and more.

"We grow accustomed to the Dark" was written in 1862 and comprises five quatrains (four-line stanzas) with Dickinson's trademark dashes and unusual capitalization. The stanzas have a **ballad meter**, giving it the feel of a song, with lines alternating from four beats to three beats (tetrameter to trimeter). Rather than following a conventional rhyme scheme, Dickinson relies predominantly on assonance— the sharing of a vowel sound though not a full rhyme—throughout the first three stanzas.

The fourth and fifth stanzas employ direct rhyming, but in different lines: "Tree" and "see" in lines two and four of the fourth stanza and "sight" and "Midnight" in lines two and three of the fifth stanza. Given her willingness to disregard other grammatical rules, it is difficult to determine whether Dickinson changed the scheme for a particular reason or simply because she wanted to. Given where the changes occur, it is possible that Dickinson is intentionally shifting her approach to reflect the change from stumbling through the darkness and hitting a "Tree/Directly in the Forehead" in stanza four to adjusting "itself to Midnight" in stanza five.

On one hand, the poem describes what it is like to leave a neighbor's house at night. When first departing, the neighbor's lamp provides enough light to get you on your way. Yet as you move further away, the light fades, leaving you in increasing darkness, waiting for your eyesight to acclimate to the night. It is uncomfortable, perhaps painful, and often frightening. Our steps are "uncertain," we grope about, and "sometimes hit a Tree/Directly in the Forehead." But with

Ballad meter {a form worth remembering}

Also known as common meter, ballad meter consists of four-line stanzas that alternate between tetrameter and trimeter, and according to Edward Hirsch, "derives from the Middle English *balade*, from Old French *ballade*, from Provencal *balada*, a dancing song." Over time it became less associated with dancing and more associated with heroic tales, such as Icelandic sagas and the English tales of Robin Hood. Many scholars believe that the ballad emerged out of the ancient epics, and thus, as Hirsch explains, "the literary ballad resonates with nostalgia for a lost oral poetry."

Learn more in Hirsch's book, *A Poet's Glossary*, page 53.

time, "Either the Darkness alters – Or something in the sight Adjusts itself to Midnight …"

With this scene in mind—the stumbling, the uncertainty, the groping, and the slow movement, it becomes clear that Dickinson's strange dashes and capitalizations are used for effect—their placement mimicking the halting steps of one making their way through darkness. The rhyme scheme, too, with its unpredictability and near misses, fits the uncertainty of the traveler's steps.

Of course, Dickinson is addressing far more than the physical phenomenon of eyes adjusting to changing light. Perhaps addressing depression or grief, the poem certainly illustrates a "dark night of the soul"—a phenomenon one could suspect a recluse like Dickinson to understand. When we are forced to walk through emotional darkness, there are times it threatens to overwhelm us and fill us with dread—when it seems no light will come again. This is reminiscent of Dickinson's poem "XIX":

> *Pain has an element of blank;*
> *It cannot recollect*
> *When it began, or if there were*
> *A day when it was not.*
>
> *It has no future but itself,*
> *Its infinite realms contain*
> *Its past, enlightened to perceive*
> *New periods of pain.*

In that short poem, Dickinson describes how pain causes us to forget the existence of everything else. It forgets all that was before and cannot imagine a painless future. Darkness can do the same. Yet with time, our sight "Adjusts itself to Midnight –/And Life steps almost straight."

John Donne
1572–1631

Best known for: Holy Sonnets, *"Devotions upon Emergent Occasions"*
"A Valediction: Forbidding Mourning"

English Metaphysical poet John Donne was born into a Catholic family in 1572 during a time of intense political and religious upheaval. Catholics were a persecuted minority in England—a cultural dynamic that shaped the course of Donne's personal and professional life. After his brother died in prison in 1893 for his Catholic faith, Donne converted to Anglicanism, but his conflicted relationship with religion characterized his poetry throughout his life. After his conversion, Donne obtained a post with Sir Thomas Egerton that enabled him to live comfortably—until he eloped with Sir Thomas' daughter, Anne More. Disowned by her family, the couple lived in poverty with their many children while Donne brought in a little money writing sonnets. During this time, Donne developed the talent and scope that would make him one of the greatest poets in the English language. Metaphysical poets are known for intense philosophical and religious contemplations explored in formal poems using elaborate extended metaphors called conceits. Donne—past master of the Elizabethan sonnet—famously crafted wholly unexpected conceits—such as two fleas biting each other as a metaphor for sexual union or kidnap and rape as a metaphor for God's pursuing love. These unexpected and often paradoxical comparisons probe profound philosophical, religious, psychological, and cosmological topics by connecting abstract ideas with concrete images and metaphors. Donne began his career as a Metaphysical poet by contemplating love and desire in earlier works like *Songs and Sonnets*, but as he aged, meditations on sexual union gave way to contemplations of spiritual intimacy. *Holy Sonnets*, written later in life, contain Donne's most subtle theological reflections.

{poem}
Holy Sonnet XIV

Batter my heart, three-person'd God; for you
As yet but knock, breathe, shine, and seek to mend;
That I may rise and stand, o'erthrow me, and bend
Your force to break, blow, burn, and make me new.
I, like an usurp'd town to another due,
Labor to admit you, but Oh, to no end;
Reason, your viceroy in me, me should defend,
But is captiv'd, and proves weak or untrue.
Yet dearly I love you, and would be loved fain,
But am betroth'd unto your enemy;
Divorce me, untie or break that knot again,
Take me to you, imprison me, for I,
Except you enthrall me, never shall be free,
Not ever chaste, except you ravish me.

{reflection}

John Donne's Startling Intimacy
by Heidi White

Universally acknowledged as one of the greatest poets of all time, seventeenth-century metaphysical poet John Donne was a divided man. His vast canon remains a mottled record of its author's internal dissonance. During his lifetime, there were two dominant personae inhabited by Donne the poet: the libertine and the cleric. In his early life and work, Donne the libertine was prominent, crafting the erotic poetry of seduction and desire that we find in "Elegies" and *Songs and Sonnets*. His middle years were transitional, offering more obscure poems, such as "Anniversaries." As an older man, however, Donne grew devout and took Holy Orders in the Church of England. The erotic verse of Donne the libertine morphed into the spiritual verse of Donne the cleric—meditations on the nature of human love gave way to contemplations of the divine.

The most famous of these late spiritual poems is a nineteen-poem series of Petrarchan sonnets, most often called the Holy Sonnets, in which Donne ponders God's divine attributes (and actions) in masterful poetic language and form. Holy Sonnet XIV is considered by some to be his masterpiece and remains one of the greatest theological poems in history. Like all Petrarchan sonnets, it is made up of fourteen lines of iambic pentameter with a rhyme scheme of ABBA CDDC EFFE GG: three rhyming quatrains and a couplet. Since Petrarchan sonnets by definition contain three tightly-constructed stanzas, the form lends itself to the development and interweaving of multiple subjects within each poem, leading to closing couplets

The Sonnet {a form worth remembering}

In his book, A *Little Book on Form*, poet Robert Hass wrote that "the sonnet is the one durable, widely used form in English poetry in the last five hundred years." A fourteen-line poem, it was invented in Italy in the thirteenth century but was especially popularized by Petrarch and Shakespeare—thus the two most popular versions of the form are the Petrarchan sonnet and the Shakespearean sonnet.

The Petrarchan sonnet is made up of an octave (eight lines), rhyming ABBAABBA, and a sestet (six lines), rhyming CDECDE. The end of the octave marks a thematic turn in the poem, or *volta*, after which the sestet will resolve the problem of the poem.

The Shakespearean sonnet includes three quatrains and a couplet, rhyming ABAB, CDCD, EFEF, GG.

Learn more in Hirsch's book, A *Poet's Glossary*, page 593.

that often ponder unexpected connections or pithy resolutions to the stanzas' varied contemplations. Donne capitalized on the form's compact versatility—as well as its widespread popularity in Elizabethan England—by writing some of his most exquisite and complex poetry in the Holy Sonnets.

It is widely known that Donne is history's premier metaphysical poet. The work of these opaque seventeenth-century poets is characterized by intense reflection on philosophical matters such as religion, love, death, and morality. Metaphysical poets used elaborate metaphors called **conceits**: long, unusual comparisons that weave throughout a poem to anchor abstract ideas to the physical world. In Holy Sonnet XIV Donne uses two conceits, both jarringly violent, to explore the nature of conversion. The first conceit is seige; the second, rape.

The poem opens with "Batter my heart, three-person'd God; for you/s yet but knock," a reference to medieval military tactics when invading armies would assault a walled city's gates with battering rams. Rather than petitioning for the gentle taps we typically associate with Jesus' famous invitation in Revelation 3:20 ("Behold, I stand at the door and knock; if any man hear my voice and open the door, I will come in to him ..." [KJV]), Donne invokes the Trinity not merely to knock, but to violently breach his entire being. The implication is one of entrenched interior defiance on the narrator's part. Donne calls his soul "a usurp'd towne, to another due," acknowledging himself to be still in thrall to a different, diabolical lord—perhaps the devil, perhaps the darker aspects of fallen humanity. In order to submit to God, the narrator begs Him to "bend/Your force, to break, blow, burn and make [him] new."

This savage imagery leads into the central three lines of the sonnet, lines seven through ten, where Donne concisely contemplates the role of human reason in conversion. According to Donne, reason is God's "viceroy"—essentially his deputy—endowed with the power to rule by proxy in the sovereign's name. Reason should "defend" Donne against the diabolical ruler within his resistant soul, but instead reason is "captiv'd," "weak or untrue," its power insufficient to the task at hand. This is Donne at his most theologically subtle. As God's viceroy, reason—in submission to God—should rule Donne's soul in God's name. Yet reason is "captiv'd," presumably by the previously mentioned diabolical lord. Thus Donne describes a soul under attack—not from external forces but internal ones. This is a soul in civil war. God "as yet but knocks" while the war rages within.

The three viceroy lines transition the poem from military language to erotic language. The second conceit is one of violent sexual conquest. In line nine, the poem leaves off its military metaphor and takes up a new one: forced marriage, even rape. Donne, the female figure in the metaphor, declares himself "betroth'd unto your enemy," and therefore begs God to "Divorce me, 'untie or break that knot again,/Take me to you, imprison me." In this conceit, the narrator is united to a dark lover and "would be loved fain" by God instead. Donne declares, however, that God must not only rescue but force himself upon the beloved prisoner in order to set him free. The poem closes with the famous couplet, "Except you'enthrall me, never shall be free/Nor ever chast, except you ravish me."

This startling final couplet provides a similar, though far more mysterious, reversal to the rape conceit in the second half of the poem that the viceroy lines offers to the military one in the first half. What at first glance appears to be a straightforward invocation to personal violation is actually a petition for restoration—a fundamental longing to be made right by a stronger, more benevolent force than entropy. Freedom and chastity is the desire of the beloved, yet he knows he will not submit to God, requiring a forced takeover of human antagonism by divine will.

Yet the poem comprises only Donne's violent petitions—not the divine response. We do not know if God answers his prayers; only that "you/s yet but knock, breath, shine, and seek to mend." Thus the poem's profound theological musings remain firmly fixed in the human realm, specifically the interior world of one internally dissonant individual. This is not a poem that speculates on God-qua-God, but on the narrator's self-acknowledged disordered longing for God. Like all great poems, however, the more particular the contemplation, the more universal it becomes. "Batter my heart, three person'd God," however disturbing on first encounter, captures not only the poet's discordant (though sincere) prayers, but our own as well.

In Holy Sonnet XIV, Donne invite us into a strange dichotomy: How can the most violent degradations of human existence possibly correspond to the holy purity of Divine Love? Holy Sonnet XIV is a poem replete with paradoxes and reversals that remind us that the human heart remains a place of dark mystery, craving to be redeemed. This is a fitting contemplation for those of us who resonate with John Donne, the libertine cleric who gave a voice to our most dissonant prayers.

Paul Laurence Dunbar
1872–1906

Best known for: "Sympathy," "Dreams,"
"A Warm Day in Winter"

The son of slaves, Paul Laurence Dunbar was a Kentucky poet, novelist, and playwright who was one of the country's first influential black poets despite a relatively brief career which was cut short by his death of tuberculosis at just thirty-three years old. Although it makes up only a portion of his canon, Dunbar was well-known for his use of "the Negro Dialect" as in poems like a "Warm Day in Winter" thanks in part to William Dean Howell, editor of *Harper's Weekly*, who championed Dunbar's dialect verse. But Dunbar also wrote skillfully in more conventional English forms, so he was not just a great Black American poet, but a great American poet, full stop. James Wildon Johnson, one of Dunbar's notable contemporaries, wrote that Dunbar was:

> *"the first poet from the Negro race in the United States to show a combined mastery over poetic material and poetic technique, to reveal innate literary distinction in what he wrote, and to maintain a high level of performance. He was the first to rise to a height from which he could take a perspective view of his own race. He was the first to see objectively its humor, its superstitions, its short-comings; the first to feel sympathetically its heart-wounds, its yearnings, its aspirations, and to voice them all in a purely literary form."*

{poem}
Sympathy

I know what the caged bird feels, alas!
  When the sun is bright on the upland slopes;
When the wind stirs soft through the springing grass,
And the river flows like a stream of glass;
  When the first bird sings and the first bud opes,
And the faint perfume from its chalice steals—
I know what the caged bird feels!

I know why the caged bird beats his wing
  Till its blood is red on the cruel bars;
For he must fly back to his perch and cling
When he fain would be on the bough a-swing;
  And a pain still throbs in the old, old scars
And they pulse again with a keener sting—
I know why he beats his wing!

I know why the caged bird sings, ah me,
  When his wing is bruised and his bosom sore,—
When he beats his bars and he would be free;
It is not a carol of joy or glee,
  But a prayer that he sends from his heart's deep core,
But a plea, that upward to Heaven he flings—
I know why the caged bird sings!

{reflection}
When a Poet Personalizes Trauma
by David Kern

One of the most influential African American poets in the American literary canon, Paul Laurence Dunbar was the son of slaves. Born in 1872, he was known during his life especially for verse written in the "Negro dialect" that his parents celebrated in the stories and songs they shared with him, but he also produced some of the finest formalist poetry of the late nineteenth-century—poetry that is on par, at its best, with the most popular poems of Robert Frost. Alas, although Dunbar was born in the same decade as Frost and Wallace Stevens, and although he displayed as much promise as they did, Dunbar didn't live to participate in the poetic reformation they helped usher in. Tragically he died at thirty-three of tuberculosis, having just entered what surely would have been the prime of his literary career. With a little luck, he could have been the Black voice of his generation. "Sympathy," the poem you find here, is the one that most carries forth his legacy, that evinces his gifting, and that gives voice to the themes he was consumed with—themes which remain meaningful 120 years later.

Today this poem is probably best remembered for its final line, "I know why the caged bird sings," which Maya Angelou famously borrowed for the title of her notable autobiography. Angelou certainly did her fair share to keep Dunbar and "Sympathy" in the consciousness of modern readers, but the poem has much to offer on its own.

Published in 1902 in *Lyrics of the Hearthside*, "Sympathy" is, as Carol Rumens wrote for the *Guardian*, "an almost unbearably painful lyric." It's at once angry and full of longing, formal and informal, old-fashioned and progressive. It attempts to give voice to the voiceless while remaining rooted in the tradition of the **lyric poem**. As

The Lyric {a form worth remembering}

The lyric, one of the oldest forms of poetry known to man, gets its name from the ancient Greeks who sang poems accompanied by the lyre. As Edward Hirsch explains in *A Poet's Glossary*, the lyric was one of three "classes" of literature identifed by the Greeks, along with the epic and the drama, and was marked by first-person voice.

In recent centuries, the lyric has often been highlighted by a deeply intimate tone, which makes it ideal for exploring the inner/spiritual life of the poet.

Learn more in Hirsch's book, *A Poet's Glossary*, page 356.

Rumens put it: "Much is left unsaid, and really ought not to need saying." Great poets can say they're angry (or lonely or sad or happy) without saying they're angry, and Dunbar is a great poet.

Of course, on the other hand, as with most lyric poems, the power of the poem is not in the mystery or in the unraveling but in the way the poem articulates specific emotions so that a universal response can be drawn out. This is a poem with a clear theme and a desired response; it is not trying to hide what it is about.

When considered as an entryway into each line of the poem, the title "Sympathy" offers some fascinating insight into the multiple layers of the poem. Six times, Dunbar declares that he "knows" what or why the caged bird does what it does and feels what it feels. And in a way, so do I. I, too, can make the connections. But his degree of knowledge isn't the same as mine. Dunbar, as the child of slaves, knows far more intimately what it means to be caged than I ever will. My knowing is intellectual; his knowing is experiential. And yet he asks that I try. The poem is a plea that I make an attempt, that I imagine what it might be like to be caged "[w]hen the sun is bright on the upland slopes/when the first bird sings ...." It's a plea that I at least imagine fear and anger so strong that I'd beat against the cage until I see my own blood on the bars— that I consider the pain that would linger even when freedom finally comes. It's a plea that I recognize and remember the songs that the caged bird sings when it longs to fly wherever and whenever it wants.

And in fact, "Sympathy" is a song in and of itself. It recalls the spirituals the slaves sang as they worked and moors those songs in the traditions of which they deserve to be a part. During the nineteenth century, the lyric poem emerged as one of the most popular forms. Wordsworth, Coleridge, Keats, Shelley, Byron, Pushkin, Tennyson, Rossetti, and other famous poets all became known for their deeply personal, intense, and lyric poems. And Dunbar, as a student of the form, would have known their work. So to give voice to slave spirituals, to present them in the dominant form of the time alongside phrasing that would be comfortable in a Romantic sonnet (with hints of dialect buried in the syntax), was a profoundly enfranchising choice.

Yet "Sympathy" is also aware of the tragedy that keeps real freedom at bay. It opens with a series of images of freedom—the sun rolling across a hillside, wind drifting through grass, a river flowing, a bird traveling along in the spring, perfume floating along—and then locks them between the mirroring lines, "I know what the caged bird feels." Dunbar makes freedom sound wonderful then juxtaposes it with the inability to experience that wonder. In stanza two, he presents images of oppression—the desperate bird beating its own wing (the cruelest bondage is punishment self-inflicted out of desperation), blood on the bars, old scars pulsing. Then in the final stanza, he offers images of exhaustion—the bird is bruised and sore, pleading and praying from "his heart's deep core." In the end, there's no hope, just recognition; no resolution, just a plea for understanding. And the stasis of the poem drives the reader into his or her own heart. What does it mean to have sympathy?

Rumens wrote that this is an "unbearably painful lyric." But isn't "Sympathy" tied to the notion of common feeling? Doesn't it demand sorrow? And isn't the first step toward community bearing one another's burdens?

Dunbar, talented as he was, embellishes the poem with numerous striking phrases and syntactical choices, but none are so recognizable (and discussed) as his use of "alas," and "ah me" at the end of line one of stanza one and line one of stanza three, respectably. These embellishments seem at first to be old-fashioned exclamations of woe (and truly they are), but upon re-reading and further contemplation, they also reveal themselves as end-stops that force the reader to slow down and recognize the human cost of what is coming. They personalize the trauma.

And they even alter the rhyme scheme and thus the way in which the poem is experienced. Instead of rhyming with the final couplet as the line would without the embellishment, the line rhymes with lines three and four. "Feels" would rhyme with "steals" but instead "alas" rhymes with "grass" and "glass." Thus the personalization alters the structure of the poem, rewriting even the scansion of the verse.

Dunbar's early demise is an ever-deepening loss, a tragedy on par, perhaps, with Byron's death except that Byron spoke for a people and a tradition that had a voice. Dunbar spoke for the inclusion of a voice long-subjugated. That's why his work is worth remembering. When we memorize and recite and contemplate his lines, we participate in the bestowal for which he pleaded and prayed and longed. There is no better way to give voice to someone than to pass along their words forever.

T. S. Eliot
1888–1965

Best known for: "The Love Song of J. Alfred Prufrock,"
"The Waste Land," Four Quartets

Thomas Stearns Eliot was probably the most important poet of the twentieth-century as well as one of the most influential literary critics of any era. Through his poems, essays, plays, and journals he was (and remains today) one of the preeminent artistic taste-makers in the history of European letters. While in college, he burst onto the literary scene with "The Love Song of J. Alfred Prufrock," still one of the most beloved poems of the era. But, of course, he is best-known for "The Waste Land", the central work of the modernist movement and one of the poems that transformed the artistic and cultural sensibilities of the post-World-War-I world. A deeply Catholic writer, Eliot's work explores the dissonance and malaise of the world around him and the faithlessness and despair he sought to combat even as it often invaded his own consciousness. Indeed, as Poetry Foundation wrote in their online biography of him, Eliot "can be seen as a deeply involved and thoughtful Christian poet in the process of making sense of the world between the two World Wars." In 1948, Eliot won the Nobel Prize in Literature and received the Order of Merit in the United Kingdom. Throughout his illustrious career, he received numerous other awards, from a Tony Award for his Broadway play, *The Cocktail Party*, to thirteen honorary doctorates from universities like Harvard and Oxford.

{poem}
Preludes

I
The winter evening settles down
With smell of steaks in passageways.
Six o'clock.
The burnt-out ends of smoky days.
And now a gusty shower wraps
The grimy scraps
Of withered leaves about your feet
And newspapers from vacant lots;
The showers beat
On broken blinds and chimney-pots,
And at the corner of the street
A lonely cab-horse steams and stamps.

And then the lighting of the lamps.

II
The morning comes to consciousness
Of faint stale smells of beer
From the sawdust-trampled street
With all its muddy feet that press
To early coffee-stands.
With the other masquerades
That time resumes,
One thinks of all the hands

That are raising dingy shades
In a thousand furnished rooms.

III

You tossed a blanket from the bed,
You lay upon your back, and waited;
You dozed, and watched the night revealing
The thousand sordid images
Of which your soul was constituted;
They flickered against the ceiling.
And when all the world came back
And the light crept up between the shutters
And you heard the sparrows in the gutters,
You had such a vision of the street
As the street hardly understands;
Sitting along the bed's edge, where
You curled the papers from your hair,
Or clasped the yellow soles of feet
In the palms of both soiled hands.

IV

His soul stretched tight across the skies
That fade behind a city block,
Or trampled by insistent feet
At four and five and six o'clock;

And short square fingers stuffing pipes,
And evening newspapers, and eyes
Assured of certain certainties,
The conscience of a blackened street
Impatient to assume the world.

I am moved by fancies that are curled
Around these images, and cling:
The notion of some infinitely gentle
Infinitely suffering thing.

Wipe your hand across your mouth, and laugh;
The worlds revolve like ancient women
Gathering fuel in vacant lots.

{reflection}
Making Meaning in the Dark
by David Kern

Originally written in 1910 and 1911 when T. S. Eliot was just twenty-two, and first published in 1915, "Preludes" marked the emergence of the man who would most change twentieth-century poetry. Although it is perhaps not as comprehensive in vision as "The Waste Land" (the poem for which Eliot is best known) nor as rich in its contemplations as *The Four Quartets*, "Preludes" nonetheless offers clear evidence of why Ezra Pound championed Eliot's early work and saw in him a talent worth nurturing. In fact, even if we think of this poem as simply the promising effort of a supremely gifted young talent who had yet to reach full creative maturity, it still is one of the most interesting, memorizable poems of its century for the way it combines both literal, observational verse with impressionistic allusion with suggestion that is meaningful more for its provocations than for its logic. And certainly "interestingness" ought to be a consideration when thinking about poems worth committing to memory.

Truthfully, I have spent a great deal of time over the last decade wondering if I know what this poem is about and contemplating whether it matters if I can name that meaning. I wonder, for example, if this poem is actually as abstract as it seems—if it is nothing but the ideas in between the images—or if it is, rather, about the embodiment of abstractions as they're experienced in real life. It is a poem that is described in various places as "fragmented" (look for this poem in any popular online encyclopedia and that word will be the first you'll find), but the consistencies in the poem suggest not that it is fragmented but that life itself is fragmented, and thus this is a poem that is obsessed with the fragments of experienced life—and the way the mind and soul of living people look to make sense of them. The poem is aware, after all, that human experience is "moved by fancies ... curled around ... images," some of which are sordid, guilty images, "flicker[ing] against the ceiling."

Presented in four unique parts, the poem is simultaneously free of convention while also moored by markers of formalism. At first glance, it is easy to miss that, while not regular, the poem does have its own formal logic. It's not simply a modernist stream of consciousness (even as it is exploring the nature of consciousness itself). The first stanza includes five sets of rhyming couplets. So "passageways" rhymes with "smoky days," and "wraps" rhymes with "scraps," and so forth. And while it's not consistently upheld line-to-line ("six o'clock" being a notable exception), stanza one is also mostly written in tetrameter. So throughout, Eliot tethers his stanzas to familiar formal modes while allowing his lines to wander at times. This is free verse in its most interesting form.

Similarly Eliot confounds our expectations thematically. Line one

("The winter evening settles down") offers a scene that appears, at first, to be a stately bit of romanticism before blowing itself up on a series of adjectives that suggest not romance or intimacy but sadness—what Marion Montgomery called the "despondent acknowledgement of isolation" in his famous essay, "Memory and Desire in Eliot's Preludes." Just as the scene is beginning to "settle down," we arrive at six o'clock and "now" emerges, a bit of timelessness that places the reader in the poem and that eliminates the distance we might have felt as an outsider to the initial scene-setting. Now begins, the poem tells us, the wrapping and the beating and the steaming and the stamping. Now emerges the grimy and the withered and the vacant and the broken and lonely. And then, as if in conclusion, the signal seen, the lamps are it. A conclusion, maybe, but undoubtedly not a resolution.

When the second stanza begins, we are surprised yet again. It's morning now— morning comes to consciousness, morning itself becomes aware of the things that make it what it is: stale smells of beer, sawdust-trampled streets, and muddy feet at coffee stands. Yet again, this is not the poem we thought we were getting. Meanwhile there are hands all over—thousands of them—raising shades, looking outside into the daylight, trying to wake up, and seeking consciousness themselves. The themes of the poem begin to emerge more clearly: As daylight comes and men put on their masks with the sunrise, how can we really know who we really are, you and I and all the others we come in contact with? We are constantly putting on masks and then opening the shades.

By now, it's no surprise that part three brings, well, more surprises.

Suddenly there's an object of the poem: "you," but the poem doesn't tell us who the "you" is. The "you" could be a lover or a friend or the reader or even the poet stepping outside himself and speaking to himself as if he has acquired a higher level of consciousness, a more profound sense of self-awareness. Eliot doesn't tell us which it is precisely. But the imprecision is the point. In its generalities, it is most suggestive, and as it slips in and out of rhyming couplet and imprecise use of the tetrameter, it pushes us into our own heads. The poem suddenly becomes more personal. Somehow the more abstract the poem gets, the more it applies to me.

Of course, just then the poem reverses course and part four begins with the word "His." The object of the poem is buried behind another undefined pronoun, an unnamed character whose soul is stretched tight across the sky, trampled by insistent feet. The violence, the loneliness, and the "despondent acknowledgement of isolation" from stanza one is back along with the confusing syntax. From the beginning of part four, it is unclear who the agent of the action is. Who is doing the stretching? Has the soul been stretched by an outside force, or did the soul choose to stretch itself? And although the poem says that it has been trampled by insistent feet, to whom do the feet belong?

Rather than a scene driven by cause and effect, we are left with a series of images, a list of impressions, a catalog of observations that the aware, conscious mind might see and try to make sense of. Indeed the poem says, the making-sense of images like these is the meaningful task and the longing of the active soul—the goal and purpose of the imagination. We make meaning in the coming dark and cling to it, or else.

But, in the end, you can only laugh; some things never change. This day is all the days, revolving again and again and again, and soon it will be six o'clock once more, and the signals will come out, and the lamps will be lit.

Poems like this have both shape and shapelessness. To suggest is to hoe and to furrow; it is to make space. And when we commit these suggestions to memory, we plant seeds. When we contemplate and live with them, we water and make something rich out of them. This is why, of course, T. S. Eliot himself was so consumed with the tradition and with the nature of language and meaning-making and the stories we tell ourselves. A poem like this helps us see what makes our collective consciousness come alive.

Modernism {a term worth remembering}

While T. S. Eliot may be the best-known of the modernist poets he certainly wasn't the first. Edward Hirsch calls Charles Baudelaire (1821-1867) the "first hero modernism" and claimed that Baudelaire "inaugurated our modernity be emphasizing what is current," thus ushering in a "movement against conventional taste." For some modernist poets, the goal was to usher in a more prorgressive age, to right the wrongs of the past, and to respond to the despair of the age. As Hirsch notes, "[t]he rallying cry was Ezra Pound's jaunty slogan, "Make it New!"

Learn more in Hirsch's book, *A Poet's Glossary*, page 387.

Rhina P. Espaillat
1932–

Best known for: Rehearsing Abscence,
*"On Hearing My Name Pronounced Correctly,
Unexpectedly, for Once," "Bilingual/Bilingüe,"*

In 1939, Rhina P. Espaillat, then seven, arrived abruptly in the United States from the Dominican Republic after her father and uncle opposed the oppressive dictator Rafael Trujillo. After a short time in Washington D.C., the family moved to New York City. Her first poem appeared in *The Ladies Home Journal* in 1948 after one of her high school teachers submitted the poem without her knowledge. She has published regularly since that time although for decades her priority was family and teaching in New York City public schools. Espaillat's first book, *Lapsing to Grace*, did not come out until 1992, but since then she has published sixteen more books of original poetry, translation, and prose, and she translated many of Richard Wilbur's poems into Spanish. She has won many honors, including the Richard Wilbur Award, the Howard Nemerov Sonnet Award, the T. S. Eliot Prize, and the Der-Hovanessian Translation Prize, as well as several awards from the Dominican Republic's Ministry of Culture.

{poem}
Bilingual/Bilingüe

My father liked them separate, one there,
one here (allá y aquí), as if aware

that words might cut in two his daughter's heart
(el corazón) and lock the alien part

to what he was—his memory, his name
(su nombre)—with a key he could not claim.

"English outside this door, Spanish inside,"
he said, "y basta." But who can divide

the world, the word (mundo y palabra) from
any child? I knew how to be dumb

and stubborn (testaruda); late, in bed,
I hoarded secret syllables I read

until my tongue (mi lengua) learned to run
where his stumbled. And still the heart was one.

I like to think he knew that, even when,
proud (orgulloso) of his daughter's pen,

he stood outside mis versos, half in fear
of words he loved but wanted not to hear.

{reflection}

Learning to Understand
by A. M. Juster

Rhina P. Espaillat is not only the greatest Dominican American poet of our time—she is one of the very best poets writing in English as well. And although Espaillat first attracted attention as a poet, she has quietly become one of our finest translators of poetry. She is the preeminent translator of Robert Frost and Richard Wilbur into Spanish and of Sor Juana Ines and Saint John of the Cross into English.

One of her most popular poems is "Bilingual/Bilingüe," which has been a favorite of high school students, particularly Hispanic young women competing in the Poetry Out Loud competition sponsored by the National Endowment for the Arts. It begins with a **heroic couplet** (iambic pentameter with exact rhyme):

> *My father liked them separate, one there,*
> *One here (allá y aquí), as if aware*

Eight more flawless couplets follow this one, each of them flowing

---

Heroic couplet {a form worth remembering}

The heroic couplet was introduced into English by Geoffrey Chaucer in *The Canterbury Tales* sometime during the late fourteenth century. A couplet, of course, is a pairing of two lines; the heroic couplet, then, is defined by the pairing of two rhyming lines, both in iambic pentameter (a line of metrical poetry that is always ten syllables long with an accent on every second syllable, such as, "Shall I compare thee to a summer's day."). William Shakespeare, John Donne, Alexander Pope, and Christopher Marlowe all employed this form to great effect in plays, poems, and translation alike.

Learn more in Hirsch's book, *A Poet's Glossary*, page 135.

---

naturally into the one that follows. With only three periods in the poem, the story proceeds as if the poet is in the room talking gently to the reader.

Despite this poem's brevity, Espaillat is weaving together two important narratives. One is a version of the timeless story of division between a proud father and a proud daughter. The second is a timely story of how people in an unsettled world become alienated by differences in language and culture.

The tone of the poem runs counter to expectations; in contemporary poetry one expects a father/daughter disagreement to have the violent emotions of Sylvia Plath's "Daddy." This poet has a very different temperament; the second and third stanzas provide a sympathetic explanation for his side of the rift:

that words might cut in two his daughter's heart
(el corazón) and lock the alien part

to what he was—his memory, his name
(su nombre)—with a key he could not claim.

When Espaillat recites this poem, the music of her rolling "r" in corazon—a sound not part of standard American English—heightens the size of the rift.

As is often the case in Espaillat's poetry, a seemingly particular situation provokes meditation about more universal concerns. In the fourth couplet, in which her father tries to close down the dialogue with a barked command, the poem escapes the tension of the moment with such a meditation. In response to the harsh language of her father ("y basta"), Espaillat responds with the gentleness of a rhetorical question:

… But who can divide

the world, the word (mundo y palabra) from
any child?

The world/word wordplay in this question also subtly reminds us of the primacy of language—without words we have no way to experience the world.

The story then continues with her father avoiding confrontation as the poet avoids it by engaging in extended covert subversion:

> *... I knew how to be dumb*
>
> *and stubborn (testaruda); late, in bed,*
> *I hoarded secret syllables I read*
>
> *until my tongue (mi lengua) learned to run*
> *where his stumbled.*

This subversion is not just ordinary adolescent petulance—it is the beginning of a future poet's commitment to a life defining the world with the magic of language.

Their disagreement over language resolves, at least in part, over time, although note the ambiguity of "I like to think":

> *... And still the heart was one.*
>
> *I like to think he knew that, even when,*
> *proud (orgulloso) of his daughter's pen,*
>
> *he stood outside mis versos, half in fear*
> *of words he loved but wanted not to hear.*

Note, too, that when the poem moves to closure, the Spanish phrase "mis versos" is not broken out in parentheses the way it is in all the previous couplets but is fully integrated into her English. There are several ways to read that unexpected feature of the poem, but perhaps the best is that it is the poet's gesture of empathy and love for her father.

"Bilingual/Bilingüe" is a powerful poem driven by genuine sentiment, but not sentimentality. It celebrates civility and cultural understanding at a time when we desperately need both.

Robert Frost
1874–1963

Best known for: "After Apple Picking," "The Road Not Taken,"
"Stopping by Woods on a Snowy Evening"

In his book, Robert Frost: *The Poet as Philosopher*, scholar Robert Stanlis wrote that:

> *"as much as we may have prized Robert Frost's poems for the technical dexterity, enchanting images, apt tropes, and deft turns of phrase, we have very imperfectly understood the ideas and beliefs that inform his work. This situation is partly of his doing ... Frost generally refrained from formal self-commentary."*

Despite this, Frost was the most popular American poet of the twentieth century—perhaps of any century. Indeed, one wonders if his popularity is tied to his mystique. His poems are certainly imbued with a sense of mystery that seems consistent with his personal and "intellectual guardedness." We do know, however, that, although he was born in San Francisco, Frost spent most of his life in New England where as an adult, he lived on a farm purchased for him by his grandfather. We know that, although he grew up in the city, he was a poet of the countryside. And we know that he remains the most lauded American poet to put pen to paper: To this day, he is the only person to receive the Pulitzer Prize four times, he won the Congressional Gold Medal in 1960, and he was named the Poet Laureate of Vermont in 1961. But ultimately Frost's canon is of such a quality that to reveal the man himself too clearly seems to miss the point.

{poem}
The Road Not Taken

Two roads diverged in a yellow wood,
And sorry I could not travel both
And be one traveler, long I stood
And looked down one as far as I could
To where it bent in the undergrowth;

Then took the other, as just as fair,
And having perhaps the better claim,
Because it was grassy and wanted wear;
Though as for that the passing there
Had worn them really about the same,

And both that morning equally lay
In leaves no step had trodden black.
Oh, I kept the first for another day!
Yet knowing how way leads on to way,
I doubted if I should ever come back.

I shall be telling this with a sigh
Somewhere ages and ages hence:
Two roads diverged in a wood, and I—
I took the one less traveled by,
And that has made all the difference.

{reflection}
Very Tricky, Indeed
by Brian Phillips

Published in 1916, "The Road Not Taken" remains one of the most familiar poems in American literature. The most frequently referenced poem in the last hundred years, it has been featured in commercials and advertisements for the Ford Motor Company, Playstation, Nicorette gum, AIG Insurance, Browning firearms, and even a 2000 Super Bowl ad by Monster.com. Lines and references from the poem have made their way into dozens of television shows, movies, and popular songs. In almost every case, the poem is used as a celebration of rugged individualism and an encouragement to go your own way, follow your heart, and carve out your own path in life. Yet Robert Frost himself said of this poem, "You have to be careful of that one; it's a tricky poem—very tricky."

Though his contemporaries like T. S. Eliot and Ezra Pound were popularizing free verse, Frost demonstrated mastery of traditional forms. He once commented, "I had soon write free verse as play tennis with the net down." Yet though his poetic forms were thoroughly traditional, the subjects therein were thoroughly modern.

Frost's own life mirrored the blend (or perhaps the collision) of stable tradition and modernist despair. Born in 1874 in San Francisco, Frost spent the majority of his life in New England. He married Elinor White, his high school sweetheart, and lived on a 30-acre idyllic New Hampshire farm. By 1915, Frost had published multiple volumes of poetry, and he was one of the most famous of American writers. Yet his family would also endure tremendous suffering, losing both their firstborn son and their daughter, Majorie. Then in 1938, his wife Elinor died and, in 1940, their son Carol committed suicide. "I'm cursed. God, if I don't believe I'm cursed," he wrote in "Home Burial." The pain and loss Frost endured stands in contrast to the simple, interlocking, almost nursery-rhyme structure and feel of his most well-known poems.

Jeanne Murray Walker observes:

> *"Poetry appears less concerned with practical communication. It seems to arise out of silence and to disappear into silence. And while it is present, it behaves as if a disruptive child has gotten hold of the word processor, wreaking havoc on normal word order and creating rhythmic patterns that focus attention on themselves. It repeats sounds for effect. It forces decent nouns and adjectives into positions in sentences they never imagined ... As a dialect, poetry appears to be impractical."*

"The Road Not Taken," however, addresses the single most practical aspect of any life: decision-making. And while the poem contemplates practical action and does so in simple fashion, we must remember Frost's caution that the poem is "very tricky."

For many readers, misunderstanding and misapplication of the poem begins before its first word. Often misidentified as "The Road Less Traveled," readers have had the tendency to recast even the poem's title according to the tenets of traditional American individualism. But the true title focuses on the road not taken—perhaps preparing the reader not for a celebration of individualism but for a contemplation of missed opportunities.

The opening stanza presents the familiar scene of a single traveler in an autumn wood, facing a fork in the road and attempting to decide which of the two paths to take. The first path is "bent in the undergrowth," making it difficult to see where it might take the traveler. The second stanza introduces the second path, describing it as "just as fair ... grassy and wanted wear," yet upon closer inspection, perhaps the two paths are "really about the same." Indeed, on that particular morning, the traveler finds both paths equally leaf-covered ("In leaves no step had trodden black"), making his choice more perplexing.

Ultimately the traveler takes the second path, hoping to discover further down that the one he chose was "the one less traveled by." He follows this path not as a defiant rejection of the well-worn path but with the intention of returning to take that other path as well. As he continues his course, however, he acknowledges that because "way leads on to way," he "doubted if [he] should ever come back." One decision leads to another, which leads to another, which leads to another. Paths have curves, forks, and obstacles, making it difficult—if not impossible—to retrace them as time passes. The reader is left to wonder, "Will the day ever come for the traveler to come back?" The concluding stanza requires particular attention to time. Everything in the poem takes place in the yellow wood at the fork and shortly afterwards while the traveler begins stepping down his chosen path. Thus having already acknowledged that the paths were "really about the same" and "equally lay/In leaves no step had trodden black," he speculates:

> *"I shall be telling this with a sigh*
> *Somewhere ages and ages hence:*
> *Two roads diverged in a wood, and I—*
> *I took the one less traveled by,*
> *and that has made all the difference."*

The paths were essentially the same, but the traveler tells himself a different story. Does that story have a happy ending? What does his "sigh" indicate? Satisfaction? Resignation? Regret? He hopes to tell that taking the road "less traveled by ... has made all the difference," but is that difference good or bad? We do not know.

The end of the poem redirects us to its title, "The Road Not Taken." Among the unanswered and somewhat mysterious questions remaining, let us add another, more perplexing one. Which road was "the road not taken"? Is Frost calling us to reflect upon missed opportunities? Or is he speaking of the road the traveler did take but speculatively—and perhaps wrongly—described as "the one less traveled by"? Very tricky, indeed.

75

{poem}
Stopping By Woods on a Snowy Evening

Whose woods these are I think I know.
His house is in the village though;
He will not see me stopping here
To watch his woods will fill up with snow.

My little horse must think it queer
To stop without a farmhouse near
Between the woods and frozen lake
The darkest evening of the year.

He gives his harness bells a shake
To ask if there is some mistake.
The only other sound's the sweep
Of easy wind and downy flake.

The woods are lovely, dark and deep,
But I have promises to keep,
And miles to go before I sleep,
And miles to go before I sleep.

{reflection}

Easy to Remember, Difficult to Forget
by Sally Thomas

Whose woods these are I think I know.
In my long memory's afterglow,
I see the words like footprints, clear
And stark across the speechless snow.

These are not the words to Robert Frost's memorable poem, though it is easy to think they are. One perhaps under-appreciated virtue of a poem as familiar as "Stopping By Woods on a Snowy Evening" is how easy it is to rewrite. It's a good exercise for the budding rhyme-smith or metrist: find words—any words—that fit the rhyme scheme and meter, plug them in, et voilà, you have, if not exactly a new or original poem, at least a pleasant parlor game. Years ago, a friend and I, both eleventh-grade English teachers, our classrooms next door to each other, used to play a version of this "Rewrite Stopping By Woods" game whenever we passed in the hall. "My little horse must think it queer," one of us would say. The other would have to respond, "To stop without a [something] near"—a pool hall, a juke joint, a ski lodge, a subway— anything that was not a farmhouse but scanned like one.

Obviously those two lines stand out in my mind, but in truth, committing the whole poem to memory to begin with wasn't hard. It came up in the textbook, and I read it aloud because it's marvelous to read aloud until I no longer had to look at the page to know what came next. By seventh period, I could rattle the whole thing off without stopping by woods or by anything else. "Stopping By Woods" is one of those poems whose surface simplicity makes it almost ridiculously easy to memorize. Its interlocking rubaiyat stanzas, with their AABA BBCB CCDC DDDD rhyme scheme, create a closed and predictable structural cosmos for the poem, handing the memorizer repeated rhymes exact to the point of inevitability. Per the rules of the rubaiyat form, the third line of each stanza acts as a prompt for the following stanza, an easy mnemonic, though in "Stopping By Woods," stanza four bends the rules, with all four of its lines ending on the D rhyme. Traditionally in this form, the third line of the final stanza would pick up the A rhyme of the first. Frost's formal choice here creates, among other things, an effect that resolves the poem with the same sort of aural emphasis that the closing couplet of a sonnet might generate, like a hammer stroke of sound. And of course, once you're there, and everything rhymes with "sweep," and the last two lines both end in "sleep"—well, there it is. The speaker is loitering in the woods, but you, so to speak, are home.

The poem's meter, too, makes it almost impossible not to memorize.

Like the rhyme scheme, it's an exercise in precision. The metronomic tetrameter, untroubled by any substitution or variation, ticks away as regularly as the meter of a nursery rhyme. There is never a moment anywhere in the poem where the words run counter to the meter, never a moment in reciting it in which you find yourself emphasizing syllables which you would never emphasize in ordinary conversation. The regularity of its cadence becomes almost soporific: a cradle rocking, a horse trotting; steady, predictable, and quieting as a lullaby. You can set the words to a tune: I've sung "Stopping By Woods" to the melody of the Gregorian chant "Jesu, Dulcis Memoria," for example, and it works. In fact, when I think of it, that's what I hear in my mind. In any event, whether you sing this poem or whether you say it like a nursery rhyme in singsong rhythm, the meter engraves the words on your brain whether you like it or not. I can't imagine wanting to forget a poem I had memorized, but I also can't imagine being able to forget this one.

But what makes this poem memorable—which might or might not mean the same thing as unforgettable—is something at once bound up with these surface patterns of rhyme and meter and infinitely deeper and more complex. For all its nursery-rhyme simplicity, "Stopping By Woods on a Snowy Evening" is not exactly a nursery rhyme. I have read it to young children for its beauty and musicality, but even so, my own ear catches the poem's stranger, darker chords. And often enough, the very elements that make the poem simple also sound those chords.

Take that final stanza, for example, the place where Frost has broken with the conventions of the rubaiyat form. Again, in the rubaiyat, the final stanza's third line would pick up the A rhyme of the first stanza so that the poem's resolution involves a return to where it began, a circle closed. And for all the emphatic finality of the repeated end-rhyme in that stanza—"deep/keep/sleep/sleep"—there is also a certain open-endedness to this ending. As tightly woven as the poem appears in terms of its rhyming framework, in the end, like the speaker himself, it seems to hesitate in its forward progress. It doesn't turn back as a traditional rubaiyat would do, but it also doesn't move on. It stops, spins its wheels, and sticks at its rhyme. It loiters, at once resolved and unresolved, closed but left ajar. Of course, the repeated rhyme in that final stanza operates almost on the level of an earworm. Once you hear them, you can't forget them. I suspect that for many people, in fact, the best way to commit the poem to memory is to begin with that stanza and work backwards, following the rhymes. Yet in the poem's closing, repetitive as it is, there's nothing simplistic any more than our own voice, returned to us in an echo in a bare stone canyon, is simplistic. It returns to us in haunting layers of sound. In "Stopping By Woods," the echoing quality of the last lines, "And miles to go before I sleep,/And miles to go before I sleep," amplifies the speaker's aloneness before the mystery of the snowy woods. And it is this quality—solitude? or loneliness? or both?—that hangs, an emotional echo, on the cold, dark air of the mind.

Meanwhile the meter plays a similarly complex role, aurally and thematically. I've noted its regularity and the fact that it can be sung as Gregorian chant. In fact, chant seems the most appropriate kind of music for this poem: legato in its delivery, without discernible dynamics, no crescendo or decrescendo, no surges or ebbs of emotion, just a calm and calming thread of sound. Or again, to recast the poem's rhythm in terms of onomatopoeia, it is the steady beat of a serene pulse, the drowsy note of trotting hooves on a familiar path. At the same time, as in the rhyme scheme, there is trouble beneath the surface, dark water under a shining veneer of ice. At the poem's formal heart lies a dissonance to disturb its tight harmony, a tension between quietness and disquiet. From its opening stanza, the poem describes the act of stopping and waiting in silence. Yet the meter keeps its implacable pace: time moving on, the universe in constant motion, and the tiny speaker in the woods caught up against his will in its machinations. I dislike overdeterminist readings of "Stopping By Woods" that cast it as a poem about suicidal ideation, for example—full stop—but there is no getting around the vein of darkness in Frost's poetry generally or in this poem in particular. Or if not darkness, then disquietude or mistrust: The universe is beautiful in its silent mysteries, but the mystery is dark at its core. The universe is unsafe, and its human citizenry remains always at its mercy. Even as human beings wish the cosmos to be one way, it reveals itself to be something else entirely—a place where in an instant, a boy's hand may be cut off in a saw or where a carrion bird shakes down snow to cleanse a day of regrets. Compared with a poem like "Out, Out—," "Stopping By Woods" is almost too easy in its beauty—almost, but not quite. It is these tensions, as between the speaker's own impulses and that of the meter, that raise its prettiness into high relief, so that it casts shadows. Its formal elements, as part of its thematic music, make it an easy poem to remember and a difficult poem to forget.

On the other hand, again, those formal elements also make it an

easy poem to play with, to toss back and forth, and to quote and mis-
quote and make a Mad Lib of, filling in the iambs. The disturbances
beneath the surface are real and compelling; they are the reason a
poem like this works its way into the pocket of your mind and weighs
there like an unspent quarter. But a quarter, if you have one, may be
taken out and spent or flipped—heads or tails?—or spun on a table-
top. A poem, once it's yours, enters into your linguistic currency. It
becomes your language. You might recite it—or you might, possess-
ing it, bring it out and play with it sometimes. You might rewrite it
for fun to see how a rubaiyat stanza works or to try your own hand
at tetrameter. Meanwhile if you are lucky and have the right kind of
friend, it can become your conversation. "My little horse must think
it queer—" Your friend lobs this serve at you as you pass in the hall
between classes. For an instant, before you return the serve, play the
game, and make the joke, the whole poem hangs in the air between
you, unspoken but belonging to you both, shared and known.

Blank verse {a form worth remembering}

Robert Frost's was one of the most prominent twentieth-century
poets who wrote in blank verse, a form marked by unrhymed
iambic pentameter. But one could argue that no line-form is
more important in the development of poetry in the English language. In the sixteenth century, the first translation of Virgil's
Aeneid was in blank verse. Shakespeare employed it exten-
sively. And Milton used it in *Paradise Lost* nearly a hundred
years later. In nineteenth century, Keats, Shelley, and Tennyson
helped make it the form in which seventy-five percent of all En-
glish-language poetry is written.

Learn more in Hirsch's book, *A Poet's Glossary*, page 73.

Dana Gioia
1950–

Best known for: ""California Hills in August,"
"In Cheever Country," "Can Poetry Matter?" (essay)

Like Wallace Stevens and William Carlos Williams before him, Dana Gioia made a professional life for himself outside of poetry before being known primarily as a writer. Whereas Stevens was an executive of an insurance company, and Williams was a doctor, Gioia worked for years as a Vice President for General Foods (where, according to various online biographers, he helped turn the Jell-O product line around). In the early 1980s, however, Gioia published a now-famous essay in *Atlantic Monthly* called "Can Poetry Matter?"—an essay that eventually became a book of the same name. Thanks at least in part to the popularity of that essay, Gioia was able to leave the business world and turn his attention to poetry and music. From 2003 to 2008, he was a chairman for the National Endowment for the Arts, and today he is the Judge Widney Professor of Poetry and Public Culture at the University of Southern California. In 2015, he was elected as the California state Poet Laureate. In short, Gioia is one of the most well-regarded poets of our time. As critic Kevin Walzer wrote:

> *"In his lyric poems, he works equally well in free verse and traditional forms, and in fact merges them in many cases; he works hard to give his metrical poems the colloquial quality of the best free verse, while his classically-trained ear gives his free verse a sure sense of rhythm that approaches a formal measure."*

{poem}
Words

The world does not need words. It articulates itself
in sunlight, leaves, and shadows. The stones on the path
are no less real for lying uncatalogued and uncounted.
The fluent leaves speak only the dialect of pure being.
The kiss is still fully itself though no words were spoken.

And one word transforms it into something less or other—
illicit, chaste, perfunctory, conjugal, covert.
Even calling it a kiss betrays the fluster of hands
glancing the skin or gripping a shoulder, the slow
arching of neck or knee, the silent touching of tongues.

Yet the stones remain less real to those who cannot
name them, or read the mute syllables graven in silica.
To see a red stone is less than seeing it as jasper—
metamorphic quartz, cousin to the flint the Kiowa
carved as arrowheads. To name is to know and remember.

The sunlight needs no praise piercing the rainclouds,
painting the rocks and leaves with light, then dissolving
each lucent droplet back into the clouds that engendered it.
The daylight needs no praise, and so we praise it always—
greater than ourselves and all the airy words we summon.

{reflection}

Praise in the Midst of Grief

by Christine Perrin

"Words" opens Dana Gioia's collection, *Interrogation at Noon*, which also closes with a short poem called "Unsaid." Thus the collection is bracketed with an inquiry about language—about what can and should be said. The closing poem declares, "So much of what we live goes on inside—," referring to grief, unacknowledged love, and "letters that we write our dead." The essential, but not singular, dead beloved in this book is the son of the poet, which we know from a poem called "Pentecost." He is referred to in another poem ("Metamorphosis") as a "gentle ghost," an "unknown companion of our spring," a "changeling," a "nightingale," a "laurel tree," and, generally, as a figure absorbed into the natural world as was Daphne—a dryad-turned-tree made safe from the god Apollo by her metamorphosis. This context is important for understanding why a poet would open a poem and a book with a claim like, "the world does not need words."

The poem claims that "to name is to know and remember," and yet the poet is skeptical of the ability of a word to adequately encapsulate all we mean or feel. He seems to be suggesting that, in the story of grief and the presence of beauty, so little can be named, and whatever is named is done so that what is beloved can be known and remembered. The speaker admits that naming a stone "jasper" or "cousin to the flint the Kiowa/carved as arrowheads" helps us to see. Thus our sight is sharpened and honed by naming, and naming becomes an activity that develops perception. But naming is also essential in praise, and the world—according to this poet—is worthy of our praise. The poem feels its way to apprehending that we are creatures whose office it is to praise—*homo adorans.* Our praise is superabundant, but that is what makes it praise and puts the world and ourselves and, perhaps, our words in proper relation.

Memorizing this open verse poem of four, five-lined stanzas will be helped by paying close attention to the argument nature of its structure. Note the opening words of each stanza: each stanza is a unit (or room) unto itself with a period at the end—it doesn't spill over from one to the next. The first stanza has a declarative statement: "The world does not need words." The second extends that beginning with "And," the third qualifies the statement with "Yet" as its first word. The final stanza reiterates the need statement but extends the original argument beyond speech to praise: "The sunlight needs no praise … and so we praise it always."

Gioia wrote the famous essay, "Can Poetry Matter?" Thirty years later, he is grappling still with that question in this poem. Thus it is a deeply personal meditation about the beloved dead as well as a corporate meditation of what art, and language in particular, might accomplish. This is an old question. Some have said that all art aspires to the condition of music. In a similar but more pessimistic vein, the collection from which this poem comes opens with an epigraph from Flaubert insisting that "[h]uman speech is like a cracked kettle on which we beat crude rhythms for bears to dance to, while we long to make music that will melt the stars." We long to make music, melt stars, and create worlds; and our tool is insufficient to those longings.

It is not an accident that stones are the central image around which this poem about words turns. In scripture, Christ says this to the Pharisees about his disciples (when the Pharisees ask Him to quiet the disciples): "I tell you that, if these should hold their peace, the stones would immediately cry out (Luke 19:40 [KJV]). Gioia wants to be quiet, perhaps, and not speak words that are imperfect, cracked, or poor names to grief and beauty, but he realizes that the stones would need to cry out if we don't. The made world (and being itself) deserves our praise, and we do this with words because they are the instrument that we have been given.

Since this poem relies so heavily on argument and sings only reluctantly, it may be hard to memorize. You might choose a memorable phrase or image for each stanza in addition to the opening and closing words. Some of the ones that grip me are "fluent leaves," "touching of tongues," "cousin to the flint," and "painting the rocks and leaves with light." But you will notice when you try to extract these bits that there is much repetition of image in the poem: kisses, leaves, sunlight, shadows, dialect, tongues, and stones keep circling round the stanzas. Certainly it's worth identifying that the last stanza arrives, however circuitously, at praise.

Richard Hayden
1913–1980

*Best known for: "The Ballad of Nat Turner,"
"Frederick Douglass," "Those Winter Sundays"*

American poet Robert Hayden was born Asa Bundy Sheffey to a poor family in Detroit, Michigan. Raised in four different foster homes, his childhood was troubled. After graduating from high school in 1932, Hayden earned a scholarship to Detroit City College (now Wayne State University). He later earned a graduate degree in English Literature from the University of Michigan where he became the first Black faculty member in the English department. In the 1930s, Hayden researched Black history for the Federal Writers Project, an endeavor that shaped his career. Along with his knowledge of history, Hayden's Baha'i faith—an Eastern religion espousing human dignity and the unity of world religions—was fundamental to his identity as a poet. Although his poetry displays deep empathy, knowledge, and solidarity with African American experience, Hayden resisted being identified as a racial spokesman. He wanted to be known as an American poet rather than a Black poet. William Meredith, in his introduction to *Collected Prose*, records that Hayden "would not relinquish the title of American writer for any narrower identity." During the tumultuous 1960s, his work was controversial for this reason. Although known as a formal poet, Hayden's poetry resists attempts to characterize it as traditional. His formal poetics provide the framework for his well-known exploration of the communal and individual American experience. It was not until the publication of *Selected Poems* in 1966 that Hayden's work earned widespread critical attention, gaining more notoriety and acclaim with each succeeding volume. By the time Hayden died in 1980 in Ann Arbor, Michigan, he was well established as a premier American poet.

{poem}
Those Winter Sundays

Sundays too my father got up early
and put his clothes on in the blueblack cold,
then with cracked hands that ached
from labor in the weekday weather made
banked fires blaze. No one ever thanked him.

I'd wake and hear the cold splintering, breaking.
When the rooms were warm, he'd call,
and slowly I would rise and dress,
fearing the chronic angers of that house,

Speaking indifferently to him,
who had driven out the cold
and polished my good shoes as well.
What did I know, what did I know
of love's austere and lonely offices?

{reflection}
The Inelegant Grace of Confession
by Christine Perrin

Sunday is a day that we expect to be different from other days. We usually don't go to work outside the home and often even our housework is put aside. Some go to church as, we can surmise from the poem, this family did. If we read only the title of this poem and nothing more, we might get a feeling of rest and fond nostalgia. Yet it takes only the first two lines to quickly see that the feeling of this poem is not what you might expect. The speaker's father is getting up early and getting dressed in "the blueblack cold." With the tiny word "too" in the first line, we know this is something he does every day, and by the third and fourth lines we know that what the father does after he rises and dresses is manual labor that makes his hands "cracked" and aching. Years or perhaps decades later, it has struck the son that no one, including himself, thanked his father for starting those fires, for getting up early, or for working a difficult job to help keep the family and household functioning.

This poem is made of three stanzas of uneven length and unmetered lines. In the first stanza, the poet has chosen to list each item of service on its own line. This adds to the sensation of it being labor and to our sense that it was a long list of acts. Line five ends the list abruptly with a **caesura** (a break in the flow of sound) that pulls the speaker out of his meditation with the bitter realization that the speaker's father was not thanked for this gift. Ending the stanza on that note leaves the reader, along with the speaker, pondering this sad thought. The white space between stanzas (called "rooms") reinforces the discomfort of this awareness.

The first stanza, as with the others, does not rhyme but still engages a multitude of sound patterns. Many long vowel sounds wind their way throughout these five lines: clothes, cold (long "o"); ached, labor, weekday, made, banked, blaze, thanked (long "a"). In addition to vowel sounds (called assonance), there are prominent consonant sounds: "c/k" (clothes, blueblack, cold, cracked, ached, week, banked, thanked) and "b" (blueblack, banked, blaze). Some consonant sounds are repeated at the beginning of words in a short succession (called alliteration) "clothes/cold," "weekday/weather," "banked/blaze." The effect of rhyme is different, more ordered, and less haphazard, but these other sound-types can reinforce the mood or feeling that is developing in the poem. They can order the poem in a way that is different from consistent, expected, echoed sound at the end of a line. The long vowel sounds tend to reinforce a sense of longing, and the hard "k" sounds harsh. This first stanza draws the portrait of the father in the context of the home. Closing the first stanza with the bald statement, "No one ever thanked him," leaves us in the moment of unhappy recognition. It communicates the sense that it is too late for thanks or to make amends either because the father is gone (perhaps he has died) or because the moment of thanks has passed.

The second stanza, another room, shifts its attention to the speaker as an adolescent who explains that by the time he woke, the heat created by his father's hands had already begun to warm the house. The speaker brings us into the experience by creating the often repeated morning scene—the cold "splintering, breaking," the father calling up the stairs to get the children out of bed, the reluctant riser "slowly ris[ing] and dress[ing]." We are surprised at the end of the second stanza when the speaker describes his fear of the "chronic angers of that house." He does not elaborate on what those angers were or how intensely they characterized the family. We know that they are important, for again he has chosen the last line of the stanza to place this piece of information, which leaves the reader in the presence of its knowledge and creates emphasis. This line is enjambed to the next (it crosses from one stanza into the next), which suggests the overflow of anger—both in terms of its role in the family as well as the impact of its presence. The second stanza uses temperature symbolically—the physical warmth and the cold of the house is a reflection of the emotional temperature of its relationships. There is coldness—indeed, later the speaker refers to his own "indifference" toward his father, which is a type of coldness—but there is also warmth of several varieties. After all, the poem is being written to commemorate the love that was shared and not entirely acknowledged. Yet there was also the warmth of anger—too much emotional heat that, like the warming fire, can singe and burn.

Perhaps the greatest beauty of this poem is its accurate portrayal of how love and hurt lie close to each other. The family life wasn't perfect—it would not be suited for greeting-card sentiment—but it is honest. It also seems to acknowledge that, despite our imperfect love for each other, the abiding reality of the exchange is the love. The sound reinforces the "angers" as well as the warmth. When an old house warms up, it creaks and shivers; the wood itself pops and breaks. But anger also splinters and breaks, so the sounds work on both a literal and a figurative level (or symbolic level, suggesting something beyond the concrete meaning). This second stanza is full of "s" sounds and "k" sounds that seem to mimic the warmth as well as the harshness.

In the third stanza, the adult speaker finishes by admitting his part in the hurt of the family, explaining his childish blindness that wasn't able to see what his father had done for the family despite whatever he hadn't done. In a climax of emotion, the speaker calls out with a voice mingled with thanks and grief, "What did I know, what did I know?" He understands now—perhaps because he himself is a father, perhaps because of the insight that time gives, perhaps because his father is gone and the speaker can now examine more closely his father's legacy—that love's offices (or the jobs of love) are "austere and lonely." "Austere" means "stern, forbidding, grave, unadorned," all qualities that we sense were true of the father.

Then suddenly we understand, as the speaker does, that these may also be qualities of love. Love's job can be stern and unfancy. The act of loving, the speaker seems to say, is not chiefly a sentiment or a warm tingling feeling, but rather it is a grave, hardworking, self-sacrificing, thankless task. It is a lonely task; sometimes you do it without being understood. The repetition of that final phrase, and the poet's choice to make it a question, gives the reader the sense of the son's anguish and regret. Once again, the stanza ends with a lingering regret, a lingering sense that this knowledge has come too late and is something the son will have to bear. The long vowel sounds have returned to this final stanza, in particular the long "o" (cold, know, lonely), which contributes to the quality of moaning.

This is powerful and moving and speaks beyond the lives of the specific individuals in the poem. Don't we all have regrets about the way we've treated those closest to us? This poem is a beautiful example of how free or open verse makes a shape and uses the line and stanza for structure, even when there isn't meter and rhyme. The decisions of where to break the lines seem governed by the dawning awareness of the speaker—he is piling up the facts of the situation, the story. Each piece of information has its own line; each piece is a kind of evidence in the court of the law of the heart. The lines aren't precisely uniform, but we can see that the first stanza establishes an average line length that basically holds for the rest of the poem.

Each stanza draws a different perspective: the father, the speaker as an adolescent, and the speaker as an adult. Each stanza ends at a place that is difficult and resonant. The last anguished question seems to be asked of the darkness.

There is something austere about the speaker's tone of voice. He presents the facts unadorned—there aren't many adjectives beyond what will communicate the necessary message. The speaker is determined to give us an accurate picture; he isn't trying to make himself or his father look better than they were—as often happens in funeral speeches, for example. From the beginning of the poem we hear regret in this voice, and there is the sense that the speaker's failure cannot be easily set right. That failure is communicated in every element of this poem, including and, perhaps, especially in its inelegant shape: the unpatterned, unrhymed lines and stanzas. The skillful use of silence in this poem also communicates the speaker's sense of failure while at the same time creating space for reverence, remembrance, and, perhaps, in some way, forgiveness.

This is a remarkably easy poem to memorize. The images guide the memory: the father's hands, the warming rooms, the shoes. The sounds guide the tongue. The emotion imprints the encircling question.

This essay was revised from an essay originally published in The Art of Poetry *by Christine Perrin (Classical Academic Press).*

George Herbert
1593–1633

Best known for: "Love III,"
"The Pulley," "The Collar"

George Herbert was the fifth son of a wealthy and influential Anglican family with aristocratic roots. His father, Richard Herbert, died when the boy was three years old, leaving his mother, Magdalen (neé Newport), a widow with ten children. Magdalen had a large fortune, a prodigious intellect, and a strong will. She was determined to raise her children to be devout Anglicans in an English culture characterized by an acrimonious divide between Rome and the Church of England. Artistic by inclination, Magdalen Herbert was a friend and patroness of John Donne and other Metaphysical poets. Donne, who dedicated his *Holy Sonnets* to Magdalen Herbert, was young George's godfather. Showing great intellectual promise at a young age, Herbert received a full classical education at Westminster School and Trinity College, Cambridge. But in 1629, he rejected both scholarly and political career opportunities to become an Anglican priest and subsequently moved to the rural parish of Bemerton where he entered the ministry and wrote poetry. Well-known as a Metaphysical poet, Herbert wrote verse characterized by deep religious devotion, formal excellence, and precise language. Like all Metaphysical poets, Herbert explored abstract ideas through the use of elaborate metaphors called conceits. Herbert's poetry is unique among the Metaphysical poets, however, in that he oriented his metaphysical contemplations toward wholly devotional matters. He often crafted his poems in a particular shape on the page so that its visual image reflected its interior themes. Herbert's career as a priest and poet was short; he died in 1633 from tuberculosis at the age of forty. His single volume of poetry, *The Temple*, was published that same year and quickly became a critical and popular success. Herbert is ranked with Donne among the great Metaphysical poets.

{poem}
Love (III)

Love bade me welcome. Yet my soul drew back
                         Guilty of dust and sin.
But quick-eyed Love, observing me grow slack
                         From my first entrance in,
Drew nearer to me, sweetly questioning,
                         If I lacked any thing.

A guest, I answered, worthy to be here:
                         Love said, You shall be he.
I the unkind, ungrateful? Ah my dear,
                         I cannot look on thee.
Love took my hand, and smiling did reply,
                         Who made the eyes but I?

Truth Lord, but I have marred them: let my shame
                         Go where it doth deserve.
And know you not, says Love, who bore the blame?
                         My dear, then I will serve.
You must sit down, says Love, and taste my meat:
                         So I did sit and eat.

{reflection}

An Inextricable Strand of Beauty
by Sally Thomas

On those occasions when I am called upon to recite a poem from memory, often the first thing my mind's clutter yields is a little epigram, the title poem in a book of comic verse my children enjoyed when they were young: "Marguerite, go wash your feet/The Board of Health's across the street." It's brief, jokey, and formally precise in the way that successful comic poems tend to be. I memorized it without even trying because my children thought it was funny. Like the punch bowl I store in the attic, this epigram is good to bring out at parties now and again, but it is otherwise kind of irrelevant. I don't know why I have it—any more than I know why I have a punch bowl—though I like it, and it is sporadically useful to possess.

Meanwhile there are poems that I actively want to know by heart—complexes of meaning and feeling which point toward larger truths. These are poems I want to contemplate as they hang shining on my mental iconostasis. They're poems that make me want to renovate the attic of my mind so that it's no longer a cluttered storage space for punch bowls and trivia but an oratory filled with icons. George Herbert's "Love (III)" is one of those poems.

Like an icon—a religious image always spoken of, incidentally, as written, not painted—"Love (III)" offers, via an intricate and stylized formal structure, a window into heaven: a vision of God's profound humility and of conversion being conformed to that same humility. Love "bade me welcome," says the speaker; the poem follows him through a trajectory of refusal, protest, and ultimately acceptance of the grace Love offers. Only in submitting to Love's servanthood—as Peter accepts Christ's washing of his feet at the Last Supper—does the sinner, the poem's speaker, enter into Love's feast. When I enter this poem, I partake of the same spiritual drama. When it hangs in my memory, I can carry it with me, always and everywhere, like a pocket-sized travel icon. It suggests a larger reality—its dialogue resonating with larger echoes. If the poem's speaker encounters God in this way, then so can, and do, I. In its small drama, enacted through its formal elements of stanza structure, rhyme, and meter, the poem opens a window through which something greater shines: God serving at the table over which He presides to which fallen human beings are welcomed with joy. To meditate on the poem through these elements is to experience, again and again, that infinite view.

In the structure of its stanzas, "Love (III)" is a study in symmetry: three sestets—three sets of two-times-three, like the Trinity on sixfold repeat—each comprising alternating pentameter and trimeter lines. These three sestets advance the poem's plot: Love inviting the speaker to be His guest; the speaker at first shyly hanging back then actively arguing his unworthiness; and finally relenting, to "sit and eat" the Eucharistic "meat" that Love urges on him. Thinking of each sestet as, perhaps, a panel in an altarpiece contributing a scene or movement to a larger narrative helps me to sketch the trajectory of the poem in much the same way that the five-point plot diagram helps me to remember what happens in *Hamlet.* If I contemplate each stanza on its own, as I might contemplate the separate panels in an altarpiece, I'm struck by the drama enclosed in its six lines. In the first stanza's choreography, Love steps forward; the speaker steps back. I imagine the speaker lurking at the door, refusing, though he is welcomed, to come inside.

Stanza two devotes itself to argument: the speaker castigates himself—"I the unkind, ungrateful"—while Love replies, unswayed, that Love made the speaker anyway. By the final stanza, Love has coaxed the speaker into the house but must persuade him that he has been invited as a dinner guest, not hired as part of the catering team. At last, at the poem's dénouement, the speaker does consent to "sit and eat." As further meditation on the poem reveals, much more goes on in each panel than this general sketch describes. Still, recalling the plot sequence with its emotional dynamics is, for me, the first step toward envisioning the poem accurately in my mind.

Within the context of each stanza, the rhyme scheme extends an invitation to enter the scene more deeply. Each sestet is composed of an ABAB quatrain and a closing couplet, a construction that mimics, in truncated form, the action of an English sonnet: the quatrain poses some conflict, while the couplet resolves it. In stanza one, the quatrain establishes the poem's central conflict. Love welcomes; the speaker refuses to be welcomed. The rhyming juxtaposition of "sin" and "in," in lines two and four, emphasizes this conflict in the speaker's mind: consciousness of his own fallen state that, as he believes, should exclude him from Love's feast. The couplet, in which Love "[d]rew nearer, sweetly questioning/If I lacked anything," sets the course for the poem's ultimate resolution. Whatever is lacking, Love will provide, even Himself in the speaker's place of shame so that the speaker may sit in the seat of honor. Stanza two, meanwhile, extends this rhetorical and thematic pattern. In lines eight and ten, even as the speaker continues to protest, the pairing of "he" and "thee" as end-rhymes prefigures the conflation of these two persons into one mind. As in stanza one, the concluding couplet resolves this round of the argument. "Love took my hand and, smiling did reply,/Who made the eyes but I?" In stanza three, lines thirteen and fifteen, juxtaposing the speaker's "shame" with Love's bearing of that "blame," extend the same idea. Love, having substituted Himself for the sinner, enables the sinner to partake of the feast of Himself as the poem's final couplet describes. While rhyme always functions as a mnemonic device, here the rhyme scheme transcends the level of sound, knitting the poem together in its thematic unity. The rhymed pairings extend the poem's resonances of meaning. As I, in memorizing, anticipate the next rhyming end-word for its sound, I find myself meditating on its sense as well. Not only the sounds but the ideas themselves, embedded in those sounds, print their indelible pattern on my mind.

Like the rhyme scheme, metrical dynamics also generate resonances of sound and meaning throughout "Love (III)." Paradoxically the very regularity of its metrical patterns lies in irregularity—its tempo shifts from line to line—an effect not unlike learning to drive a stick-shift car. The constant stops and starts and jerks are unsettling even when I know they're going to happen.

Of course, the organization of the stanzas around these shifts—a regular pattern, however startling—reinforces the poem's framework as a dialogue. Two voices speak: the obdurately self-effacing "I" and generous Love, who parries the speaker's every attempt to condemn himself. This dialectical structure is echoed in the poem's metrical framework. What is chiefly notable about this relationship of sense and sound, however, is that the two might have fallen together far more tidily than in fact they do. In a more predictable poem, one voice might speak in pentameter, the other in trimeter. Instead, in "Love (III)," the speaker's voice, particularly in the first two stanzas, cuts across the metrical pattern in a kind of counterpoint. It is as if the meter contributed one harmonic line, moving forward in its alternating patterns, pentameter followed by trimeter and so on. In a second harmonic line, the speaker's voice spills over line breaks in uncontained anxiety and self-blame: "I the unkind, the ungrateful? Ah, my dear/I cannot look on thee." For much of the poem, as in polyphony, these two melodies operate independently of one another. By the middle of stanza three, however, this counterpoint has begun to resolve into a single melodic line. Like the metrical motion itself, the relationship between the *dramatis personae* is not static but full of shifts. From the beginning, in contrast to the speaker, Love has spoken His lines in harmony with the meter: "You shall be he ... Who made the eyes but I?" But by the poem's end, the speaker's previously voluble voice has contracted, too, to trimeter utterances. His surrender forms the quiet, resolving chord that ends the poem: "So I did sit and eat." This resolution echoes the poem's larger resolution: the speaker has united his voice, his mind, and his whole self to Love.

Metrical substitutions within the lines extend this sense of counterpoint, which underscores the poem's thematic choreography. In both the pentameter and trimeter lines, the iamb is the prevailing foot. Of the poem's nine pentameter lines, six of them—lines three, five, seven, eleven, fifteen, and seventeen scan unambiguously as sets of five iambs. Of the trimeter lines, all but line two—"Guilty of dust and sin"—scan similarly as regular sets of three. This is a regular enough occurrence to establish a metrical contract, a set of expectations for how the patterns of rhythm will play out. Interestingly the first two lines of the poem begin not with iambic feet, but with trochees: stressed syllables followed by unstressed. Though line one can scan as regular iambic pentameter, the effect feels a little too metronomic, too unlike a living voice. For the sake of initial memorization, I might say, "Love bade me welcome. Yet my soul drew back," if strict observance of meter helps me to get the words superficially right. But when I recite the poem aloud to meditate on its meaning, that line sounds like this: "Love bade me welcome." Spoken aloud, the line almost has to begin with either a trochee or a spondee, not an iamb, in order to make sense. "Love," as the subject of the opening sentence and indeed the whole poem's subject, demands a stressed syllable, even as the expected meter suggests otherwise. Line two, likewise, begins with a stressed syllable as if the speaker meant also to emphasize the gravity of his own state. Beginning as it does with these metrical substitutions, the poem establishes a note of discord that reflects its action: Love inviting and the speaker withdrawing and protesting.

Similar variations recur throughout the poem and, again, underwrite its emotional trajectory. Interestingly these variations consistently occur in the speaker's own voice. "I the unkind, ungrateful," he cries in line nine, the initial trochaic foot with its leading emphasis reinforcing the outburst of self-loathing. An iamb follows the initial trochee; the reading ear naturally wants to hurry over those juxtaposed unstressed syllables to the next stress. By the end of line nine, the voice has spent its emotion, and the line settles again into regular iambic feet. Throughout the poem, by contrast, when Love speaks and acts, He does so in perfect accord with the demands of the set meter. As the speaker, too, falls into line with the meter, this resolution echoes his putting-on of Love's own mind, the moment when at last he assents to "sit and eat." As with events in rhyme, the resolving of the poem's counterpoint into a single note re-enacts the central drama every time I look upon it in my mind. Like the rhyme scheme, this metrical counterpoint and resolution underscores the poem's thematic drama. Again, its complicated music invites me into the heart of its meaning.

From beginning to end, the intricate metrical musicality of this poem heightens its emotional drama and forms an inextricable strand of its beauty. If, like me, you want to remember this poem, it is precisely because these complex patternings of sound and meaning— with all their echoes, shifts, and changes—work together toward an ultimate unity. "Love (III)" is an icon to hang in the mind, and it is through all these elements, with every remembering, that the icon is written anew.

Homer
c. 1200–800 BC

Best known for: the Iliad, *the* Odyssey

Alas, virtually nothing is known about the life of Homer. He was born between the twelfth and eighth centuries BC, perhaps somewhere in Asia Minor. Tradition says he was blind, but that is likely a legend born from the appearance of the blind bard, Demodocus, in Book VIII of the *Odyssey*. We know nothing of the circumstances of his life nor his marital status, political beliefs, or social standing. Many have tried to discover more, but Homer remains shrouded in mystery. What we do know is the supreme quality of his work. Like Shakespeare—another masterful author whose personal life is an enigma—the clearest picture we have of Homer is not his personality but his genius. The *Iliad* and the *Odyssey* endure not only as the greatest epics ever written but also as the most influential narratives in Western Civilization aside from the Bible. In fact, these epic tales are so superlative that many modern scholars have speculated that perhaps Homer may not have existed at all—that he was merely a fictional persona imposed upon a written collection of cumulative oral tradition. Another theory is that Homer was more like a scribe—that he recorded the stories that were passed down over centuries of spoken narratives. Whoever Homer was (or wasn't), we know that the ancient philosophers in Athens wrangled endlessly over the content of his tales, much as we do today, and they seemed to believe that he was a flesh-and-blood man. It is difficult not to sense the shadowy figure of a mastermind of subtle genius lurking behind the cohesive tales. Although we do not know Homer as an individual, we know him as a teller of some of the greatest stories in world history. The brief selections you find in this volume offer a small glimpse at his genius.

{poem}
The *Iliad:* Book 1, lines 1-14 (trans. by Alexander Pope)

Declare, O Muse! in what ill-fated hour
Sprung the fierce strife, from what offended power
Latona's son a dire contagion spread,
And heap'd the camp with mountains of the dead;
The king of men his reverent priest defied,
And for the king's offence the people died.

For Chryses sought with costly gifts to gain
His captive daughter from the victor's chain.
Suppliant the venerable father stands;
Apollo's awful ensigns grace his hands
By these he begs; and lowly bending down,
Extends the sceptre and the laurel crown
He sued to all, but chief implored for grace
The brother-kings, of Atreus' royal race

A note about translations

Because of Homer's wide appeal and deep influence, scholars of every generation have translated his works. For this project, we have chosen two: Alexander Pope, whose elegantly stylized translation of the *Iliad* lends itself to easy memorization of the prologue, and William Cowper, whose visceral blank verse translation of the *Odyssey* is suited to the stirring nature of the passage we chose.

Epic {a form worth remembering}

Edward Hirsch defines an epic as "a long narrative poem, exalted in style, heroic in theme." The *Iliad* and the *Odyssey* by Homer are, of course, the most famous examples of the form, which is one of the reasons we chose to include them in this book. But nearly every culture has had its own version of the form, and many of them are quite well-known and worth memorizing. From the *Mahabjarata*, a Sanskrit epic from ancient India, to the Bablylonian epic of *Gilgamesh*, to the epics of the middle ages like *Beowulf* and *The Song of Roland*, the epic poem captures not just the legends of ancient cultures but also explores the psyches of those cultures, helping us understand what bound their collective imaginations. As Hirsch wrote, the epic "binds people to their own outsize communal past and instills a sense of grandeur."

Learn more in Hirsch's book, *A Poet's Glossary*, page 208.

{reflection}
Setting the Stage
by Heidi White

Like all epics, the *Iliad* begins *en media res*, or "in the middle of things." By the time the action of the *Iliad* commences, the Trojan War is in its tenth year. The Greek army has been encamped at the walls of Troy for nine years, they have failed to breach the Scaean gates, and the status quo indicates no sign of changing. Helen, wife of the Spartan king, Menalaus, remains inside the walls of the city in the arms of her lover, Paris, prince of Troy, and the mighty heroes of both sides have not engaged each other in a battle for many years.

It can be disorienting to enter the story so late in the timeline of the war. But Homer is an obliging poet who kindly encapsulates the essence of the story within the first line. With eloquent simplicity, he begins his tale by invoking a goddess to help him tell the proper story. In this context, the goddess is the muse of epic poetry, Calliope, considered by ancient authors to be the greatest of all of the nine muses (the sister goddesses who inspired mortals to create art to sing of the greatness of the gods). The invocation is particularly beguiling to the elevated style of the translation we chose—that of eighteenth-century poet Alexander Pope. This formal translation is written in heroic couplets: two consecutive rhyming lines in iambic pentameter. Although the translation may feel inordinately stylized over the course of the entire epic, it is conducive to memorization due to its unique musicality and elegant language. In Pope's flowing style, the opening line implores the muse Calliope to anchor the epic to what is perhaps an unexpected tether.

The wrath of Peleus' son, the direful spring
Of all the Grecian woes, O Goddess, sing!

With this crucial appeal, Homer bequeaths to his readers the interpretive key of the entire epic. The *Iliad* is not, after all, an epic about the events of the Trojan War. The war, with all its complexity, is simply the context or backdrop of the real story, which is something more human, more mundane: the rage of Achilles. The *Iliad* is at heart the unfolding story of the ebb and flow of one man's tumultuous wrath. About this, there is much to contemplate in the ensuing narrative.

But that is not all that the opening lines of the *Iliad* offer. The first fourteen lines constitute a prologue, which is a supremely useful literary device in the epics. The epics are long and complicated. A prologue presents narrative context and interpretive tools for the complex, sweeping epic tales. A typical prologue is made up of several pithy, significant lines of introduction that relate a condensed version of the story as well as relevant background information that orients readers to the entry point of the narrative. Since epics begin *en media res*, prologues give us clues to the past and insight into the future. In this case, the prologue tells us that the Greek king Agamemnon and the mighty warrior Achilles are at odds over a plague in the Greek camp sent by the god Apollo to punish Agamemnon for impiety. This, we learn, is the catalyst for the rage of Achilles, and thus the proper beginning of the epic tale.

Epic prologues do not merely relate elements of plot, however. Every word of an epic prologue is significant, offering insight into the wider contemplations of human existence explored throughout the epics. Although the *Iliad*'s prologue is only fourteen short lines, it is masterfully crafted to illuminate both plot and thematic elements for readers who are about to delve into one of history's greatest literary achievements. Memorizing the prologue of the *Iliad*, therefore, is more than a mental exercise. Rather, memorizers internalize a microcosm of the entire epic that anchors them to the heart of the work as they read it. It is a guide—a tether—that always leads them home. For those not reading the entire epic, memorizing the prologue is still valuable because it encapsulates the profundity of one of literature's masterpieces.

In the *Iliad*'s prologue, we discover in Achilles' "that wrath which hurled to Pluto's gloomy reign / The souls of mighty chiefs untimely slain." In terms of plot, we immediately learn that Achilles' anger will cost the Greeks countless losses. This is curious, of course, because Achilles himself is a Greek. Upon a cursory reading, it would seem that the primary outlet of Achilles' rage is his magnificent aristeia, or glorious battle, which spans Books XVII–XXII, resulting in the massacre of Trojan enemies, including the famous death of mighty

Hector, prince of Troy. Yet the prologue emphasizes the internal cost of Achilles' rage, a point worth careful reflection. According to the all-important prologue, Achilles' rage is self-destructive; it results in grievous losses to his own comrades and well-being while at the same time serving as the catalyst to the war's fated conclusion. It is Achilles' rage that breaks open the lengthy stalemate and leads to Greek triumph, yet it is also the cause of the calamitous destruction of his own forces, including a friend particularly dear to him. Thus even within the prologue, we identify the fault lines of Greek society that are further exposed in the episodes to come.

Another essential phrase in the prologue is found in line five when Homer assures us that "such was the sovereign doom, such the will of Jove." The mysterious interaction between gods and men is fundamental to the *Iliad*. Divine fate and human agency are inextricably entwined throughout the epic, with the wrath of Achilles always at the center. Yet it is not Achilles who controls the outcome of the war but Jove who decrees a Greek victory. All of the complex machinations of divine and human characters throughout the epic lead relentlessly to the inevitable conclusion put forth in line five: "such was the sovereign doom." The intermingling of fate and free will is in continual flux, but always, the prologue reminds us, in subjection to ultimate divine will.

The *Iliad* is an epic of such power and subtlety that you can read it for a hundred years and still discover something wholly new. The prologue, though brief, offers essential anchor points for interpreting the entire narrative. The keys unlock the world of the story, leading to worthy speculations from within the heart of the epic narrative. Was

Achilles' rage justified? Should Achilles have gone back into battle after the embassy in Book IX? Whose fault was Patroclus' death? Is everlasting glory worth a short, unhappy life? Do Hera's multitudinous manipulations impact the outcome of the story? How is Achilles' rage resolved? Does the *Iliad* have a happy ending? Anchored by the tethers offered in the essential prologue, these questions lead to rich contemplations of the universal questions at the heart of the *Iliad*.

{poem}

The Odyssey: Book XXIII, 208–230 (trans. by W. Cowper)

So spake she, proving him, and not untouch'd
With anger at that word, thus he replied.
  Penelope, that order grates my ear.
Who hath displaced my bed? The task were hard
E'en to an artist; other than a God
None might with ease remove it; as for man,
It might defy the stoutest in his prime
Of youth, to heave it to a different spot.
For in that bed elaborate, a sign,
A special sign consists; I was myself
The artificer; I fashion'd it alone.
Within the court a leafy olive grew
Lofty, luxuriant, pillar-like in girth.
Around this tree I built, with massy stones
Cemented close, my chamber, roof'd it o'er,
And hung the glutinated portals on.
I lopp'd the ample foliage and the boughs,
And sev'ring near the root its solid bole,
Smooth'd all the rugged stump with skillful hand,
And wrought it to a pedestal well squared
And modell'd by the line. I wimbled, next,
The frame throughout, and from the olive-stump
Beginning, fashion'd the whole bed above
Till all was finish'd, plated o'er with gold,
With silver, and with ivory, and beneath
Close interlaced with purple cordage strong.
Such sign I give thee. But if still it stand
Unmoved, or if some other, sev'ring sheer
The olive from its bottom, have displaced
My bed—that matter is best known to thee.

{reflection}

The Olive Tree Bed
by Heidi White

In Homer's magnificent epic, the *Odyssey*, our hero, Odysseus, King of Ithaca, journeys home after two decades of war and travail. The twenty-four book epic is the story of Odysseus' homecoming to his native land and of his reunion with his wife, Penelope, and their son, Telemachus, who has never known his father. Odysseus has not seen his home or family in twenty years. In that time, he has experienced many adventures and endured many hardships—battles, monsters, seductive goddesses, shipwrecks, vengeful gods—while Penelope, who does not know if her husband is dead or alive, waits. Meanwhile a group of violent and debauched suitors occupy the palace. These dissipated young men court the queen and plunder Ithaca's riches. They take over Odysseus' home and feast on his meat, drink his wine, mock his son, sleep with his servant girls, and woo his wife.

By the time Odysseus finally arrives home, slaughters the suitors, and restores the kingdom, he and Penelope have been separated for two decades. During that time, Penelope has remained faithful, weeping endless tears for her lost husband. In the midst of her grief, however, she rules Ithaca and her household capably while raising their son wisely. To rebuff the relentless suitors, she implements cunning plans to keep them at bay, showing herself in every way equal to her courageous and strategic husband. Often called "wise," "quiet," or "circumspect" Penelope, she is the icon of the faithful wife, maintaining steadfast, womanly virtue in the face of hardship and uncertainty.

When the long-suffering couple are finally reunited in Book XXIII, readers expect a satisfying reunion. Instead, Penelope resists Odysseus, unsure if the man before her is an illusion—perhaps he is a god attempting to deceive her into breaking her vows. Both Telemachus and Odysseus challenge her hesitancy. "My mother! ah my hapless and my most/obdurate mother! Wherefore thus aloof/shunn'st thou my father?" reproaches Telemachus while Odysseus cries, "Penelope! The gods themselves have giv'n/of all thy sex, the most obdurate heart." But wise Penelope refuses to be baited. She must be sure. "But if indeed/he be Odysseus, and have reach'd his home/I shall believe it soon, by proof convinced/of signs known only to himself and me." In this final display of her patient sagacity, the queen will not rush into the arms of Odysseus before she is certain, so she puts him to the test.

Calling their servant woman, Penelope instructs her to move the couple's bed from her private chamber into the public area for the man to sleep upon. Overhearing this command, Odysseus responds angrily, delivering the famous speech you are memorizing here. At the same time forceful and tender, Odysseus thunders to his wife that the bed cannot be moved. He built it himself, he declares, wrapped around a sturdy olive tree. In fact, as a bridegroom he built the entire bedchamber for his bride around that mighty olive tree in the center of his home. Their marriage bed, firmly anchored by the man himself to the rooted olive tree, abides at the heart of Odysseus' kingdom.

Odysseus and Penelope's olive tree bed is more than a clever device to test the man's identity; it is a powerful objective correlative to the couple's indomitable marriage. "For in that bed elaborate, a sign,/a special sign consists," says Odysseus. Just as the bed remains fixed at the geographical center of Odysseus' palace, so does his marriage endure as the anchoring love of Odysseus' embattled life. Penelope has spent twenty years sleeping alone in that bed, weeping for her absent husband, refusing to give herself to another man. Meanwhile Odysseus has been kept from the arms of his beloved bride, withstanding countless hardships and resisting multiple temptations to abandon his homeland and acquiesce to false homecomings far from his native land. And that whole time, Penelope was the sole occupant of the immovable bed, symbolizing the steadfast commitment of each spouse in their extraordinary marriage.

By extension, the bed is also the stabilizing force of Ithaca itself. With an absent king, the kingdom is in constant danger. Penelope, although a prodigious leader in her own right, is, after all, a woman in a man's world, and Telemachus is only a boy. Ithaca is vulnerable. The suitors are not merely a threat to Odysseus' family but to his kingdom. If even one suitor can seduce the queen and silence the heir, Ithaca is doomed. But Penelope resists the suitors. The royal marriage remains anchored with the olive tree bed, preserving the kingdom intact. As Odysseus declares, "It might defy the stoutest in his prime/ of youth, to heave it to a different spot." The suitors failed to tempt the queen from her marriage vows, and the olive tree bed remains the rooted hope of the fragile kingdom.

From a wider perspective, Penelope and Odysseus' bed has become a universal symbol for the indissoluble nature of the marriage covenant. Just as Odysseus firmly anchored the hand-hewn bed to the geographical landscape of his kingdom, so do we intentionally tether the sacrament of marriage to the rhythms of quotidian life in order to build our marriages to be sheltering bulwarks in a precarious world. Because Odysseus and Penelope both carried the precious secret of their olive tree bed, they were able to find and to heal each other at the proper time.

Upon hearing his impassioned speech, Penelope at last acknowledges the stranger as her husband. The olive tree bed was their secret; a false Odysseus would not know the secluded intimacy of their marriage bed. And so, "weeping she ran/direct toward him, threw her arms around/the Hero, kiss'd his forehead." This is the moment of true restoration for Odysseus; all of his escapes and triumphs have led to this reunion in his bride's welcoming arms. "So saying, she awaken'd in his soul/pity and grief; and folding in his arms/his blameless consort beautiful, he wept."

Odysseus and Penelope are enduring icons of marriage's redemptive potential for tenderness and strength in the midst of adversity. Although beset by relentless dangers and temptations, the lovers reunite in one another's arms. "Thou shalt to bed at whatsoever time/thy soul desires," invites reserved Penelope. "Since the immortal Gods/give thee to me and to thy home again." And so Book XXIII ends where their marriage began—in the olive tree bed—the beating heart of Ithaca, of faithful Penelope, and of great-souled Odysseus himself.

Gerard Manley Hopkins
1844–1889

Best known for: "God's Grandeur,"
"Pied Beauty," "As Kingfishers Catch Fire"

English poet Gerard Manley Hopkins was born in Stratford, Essex to a middle class family. The oldest of nine children, Hopkins grew up in a literary household. His father was a poet and novelist, and his mother was fond of reading. As a child, Hopkins was prone to behavioral extremes, once abstaining from drinking liquids until his tongue turned black, and he fainted in the schoolyard—launching a lasting tendency to rigorous asceticism. He wrote his first poetry in 1860. Hopkins studied classics at Balliol College, Oxford, forming influential lifelong friendships with poet Robert Bridges and tutor Walter Pater. Although baptized in the Anglican church he converted to Catholicism in 1866. A zealous young convert, Hopkins began studies to become a Jesuit priest, burning all of the poems he had composed before his conversion. "I am resolved to be a religious," he declared. Hopkins did not write another line of poetry for seven years. Prone to bouts of severe depression, Hopkins felt a continual internal dissonance between his vocation as a priest and his inclination to be a poet. At the request of his superior, he composed a poem in 1875 that was eventually rejected for publication. After that, moved by his longing for poetic language and forms, Hopkins wrote poetry once again but privately. When his work was published posthumously, it was universally recognized as magnificent. Hopkins left a permanent imprint on the landscape of poetic composition by subverting the traditional forms used by the staid Victorian poets. Denouncing them as "same and tame," Hopkins invented the famous "sprung rhythm" that was his own union of vivid descriptive language with Middle English poetic techniques. Hopkins died in 1889 of typhoid fever with no inkling that he would be known as a defining voice in English poetry.

{poem}
God's Grandeur

The world is charged with the grandeur of God.
    It will flame out, like shining from shook foil;
    It gathers to a greatness, like the ooze of oil
Crushed. Why do men then now not reck his rod?
Generations have trod, have trod, have trod;
    And all is seared with trade; bleared, smeared with toil;
    And wears man's smudge and shares man's smell: the soil
Is bare now, nor can foot feel, being shod.

And for all this, nature is never spent;
    There lives the dearest freshness deep down things;
And though the last lights off the black West went
    Oh, morning, at the brown brink eastward, springs —
Because the Holy Ghost over the bent
    World broods with warm breast and with ah! bright wings.

{reflection}

A Call to Behold
by Jessica Hooten Wilson

When I consider memorizing poetry, I turn first to Gerard Manley Hopkins, for his verses are beautiful, rhythmic, and rhyming. They have interjections of emotion, memorable images, and a depth of meaning, which continues to teach with every recitation. Although Hopkins died in 1889 in Ireland, his poetry sounds modern rather than Victorian. He was born into the Anglican Church but felt convicted to leave his childhood faith for the Roman Catholic Church and eventually became a Jesuit priest. He began as an artist, sketching nature, but ultimately became a poet who saw the supernatural stressed within the natural. His poetry was dedicated to God. If Hopkins feared the poems detracted from devotion, he would destroy them. While contemporary writers lament that Hopkins could not free himself from the restrictions of religion to enjoy the license of self-expression, devout believers memorize his words with gratitude and adoration that he surrendered his art to something higher and eternal. We are the recipients of his gift.

Considered one of his Wales sonnets, "God's Grandeur" was composed in 1877 during the Lenten season while Hopkins was at the Jesuit college near Clwyd studying for the exams that would assess whether he was prepared to hear confessions. To open his biography of Hopkins, poet Paul Mariani quotes the first line of "God's Grandeur": "The world is chárged wíth the grándeur of God." Hopkins believed, according to Mariani, that "[a]ll that was wanting ... was the beholder. And when the beheld and the beholder once met, when the essential nature of the thing was instressed upon the eye, ear, tongue, and mind, the heart could not help but rise up as at a sudden unheard symphony, a dance." What the reader experiences in "God's Grandeur" is the charge or command made by God to attend to the grand world he has created. Hopkins upholds its beauty for the reader in the images that he lists.

Readers will notice the stresses that Hopkins places over words, emphasizing his "sprung rhythm." Unlike the iambic meter that had been popular since Shakespeare, Hopkins returns to a meter that echoes Old English such as might be found in Beowulf. For Hopkins, his sprung rhythm more closely resembles human speech. Even those unfamiliar with poetry find Hopkins' meter easy to read. Because Hopkins enjambs his lines, readers should pause only at sentence breaks or where punctuation demands it. Other than that, Hopkins intends readers to read, for instance, "It gathers to a greatness, like the ooze of oil/Crushed" in one breath.

Sprung rhythm {a term worth remembering}

Gerard Manley Hopkins' name for a rhythm that was, as Edward Hirsch writes in *A Poet's Glossary*, consumed primarily with accents and not syllables. Hopkins hoped to create verse that approximated the musicality of human speech. He wrote that he used sprung rhythm "because it is the nearest to the rhythm or prose, that is the native and natural rhythm of speech, the least forced, the most rhetorical and emphatic of all possible rhythms." His mastery of the form and the musicality that results from it, make Hopkins one of the most memorizable poets to write in English.

Learn more in Hirsch's book, *A Poet's Glossary*, on page 607.

The poem is a Petrarchan sonnet, meaning the first eight lines (octave) form one set, and a turn (*volta*) occurs in the next six lines (sestet). In the octave, Hopkins claims that God's grandeur charges everything; "charge" here means both a command as well as electric current. The next two lines explain in images how God's grandeur charges: "It will flame out, like lining from shook foil" or "It gathers to a greatness, like the ooze of oil/Crushed." Mariani describes the first charge like Paul being blinded at Damascus whereas Augustine experiences the more gradual gathering-in by God's grandeur. In response to God's charge, men poorly respond, and Hopkins asks an accusatory question: "Why do men then now not reck his rod?" When memorizing this question, attend to the strange juxtaposition of "then" and "now" as well as the two spondee feet "men then" and "now not." Hopkins emphasizes each word—each simple, one syllable word—so that his reader will slow down.

Although the question is dense and stressed metrically, the answer following draws out syntactically—repeating, linking together clauses, listing verbs, and ending with confinement. The answer begins with a polysyllabic abstract word contrasting with the previous question: "Generations." These "[g]enerations" have trod" (Hopkins writes the verb three times). Trod, the past tense of tread, is a verb associated with treadmills, with slow going or going nowhere. The next two lines are similarly repetitive: they begin with the conjunction "And," repeat sounds in the verbs in the vowels (assonance) internal to the line, and employ consonance in the prepositional phrases or transitive objects. Hear the assonance of line six: "seared," "bleared," and "smeared" and in line seven: "wears" and "shares." Notice the repeated "s", "w," and "t" of "seared with trade" and "smeared with toil." The "s" continues repeating in line seven: "smudge," "shares," "smell," and "soil." The last line changes alliteration from "s" to "f": "foot feel," ending with the rhyme.

In addition to all of the internal rhyming, each line ends with a simple rhyme, meaning one syllable, following this pattern: AB-BAABBA CDCDCD. When I was a student, labeling these patterns intimidated me, but seeing them now strikes me as empowering, noticing how the lines lace together. The rhyme represents a colored strand woven with others to create this pattern. In this sonnet, the pattern reveals how to read which lines in tandem. Even without a formatting break between lines one through eight from lines nine through fourteen, the structure exists within the words themselves. And we may read the sestet as a thematic response to the concern posed in the octave. The turn occurs in the transition in line nine:

"And for all this." If the poet was writing prose, he would have remarked, "Despite all this," but the words "And for" tie us to the octave by repetition—the conjunction "And" was used in lines six and seven, and the sounds "or" and "f" sounds were used line eight.

The sestet offers hope. The "charge" mentioned in the beginning is recontextualized as credit and is "never spent." Whether or not the beholder attends to the flame and shine of God's grandeur, still there "lives the dearest freshness deep down things." Readers will hear the spondee* "deep down" as though Hopkins forces readers to dig deeply themselves. Then in contrast, he lifts up the gaze to the "last lights off the black West," changing color and direction in the next line to "brown brink eastward." As far as the west is from the east. In light of this hope, Hopkins marks two interjections, first "Oh" in line twelve followed by "ah!" at the end of line fourteen; he compels his reader to become a beholder—to read the feelings one should emit when seeing the world so charged.

In the final image, Hopkins compares the Holy Ghost to a mother bird. Line thirteen sounds as though it refers to creation when the Spirit hovers over the waters, but Hopkins transforms the image. Rather than hover, the Spirit "broods" like a mother. This maternal image alludes both to the God of the Old Testament and Jesus Christ in the New Testament. In Isaiah 66:13 (NIV), God speaks to Israel, "As a mother comforts her child, so will I comfort you," and Jesus alludes to this promise in the Gospel of Matthew when he exclaims, "How often would I have gathered thy children together even as a

---

*A spondee is a poetic foot consistening of two equally accented syllables.

hen gathereth her chickens under her wings" (Matt. 23:37 [KJV]). In this image, Hopkins ties the Trinity all together in the Holy Ghost "over the bent/World broods with warm breast and with ah! bright wings." Just as the sonnet began with light imagery, so it ends with "bright"-ness.

Notice the play on consonants back and forth between "b" and "w" at the start of nearly every word in the last two lines. These consonants dominate the last four lines: "black West went" and "brown brink eastward." Hopkins' poems often sound like tongue twisters when you first read them with the repetition of vowel sounds, alliteration, and internal and end-line rhymes. One must practice reading each line slowly—attending to each sound, the meaning of each word, and the connotations, denotations, and emotions that Hopkins evokes. By writing so uncharacteristically, Hopkins trains the reader to become the very beholder that he finds wanting in the world. The poem then laments the lack of a beholder and supplies it when the poem is read. To memorize "God's Grandeur" is to participate in it and to shine forth and gather to a greatness all at once.

{poem}
As Kingfishers Catch Fire

As kingfishers catch fire, dragonflies draw flame;
As tumbled over rim in roundy wells
Stones ring; like each tucked string tells, each hung bell's
Bow swung finds tongue to fling out broad its name;
Each mortal thing does one thing and the same:
Deals out that being indoors each one dwells;
Selves—goes itself; *myself* it speaks and spells,
Crying *What I do is me: for that I came.*

I say more: the man justices;
Keeps grace: that keeps all his goings graces;
Acts in God's eye what in God's eye he is—
Christ—for Christ plays in ten thousand places,
Lovely in limbs, and lovely in eyes not his
To the Father through the features of men's faces.

{reflection}

The Fundamental Attachment That Defines Us
by Maurice Manning

My first encounter with the poetry of Gerard Manley Hopkins came in a standard college survey course. I recall we read "God's Grandeur" and "The Windhover," both poems that perceive the creative force alive and present in creation and are probably the two Hopkins poems that continually show up in college textbooks, reducing his output to a thumbnail of relevance. "As Kingfishers Catch Fire" is lesser known, a poem that rarely appears in anthologies and textbooks.

I first learned of this poem two years out of college because the first line introduces a book that has mattered much to me through the years. I was teaching GED and adult literacy in rural Kentucky for the Christian Appalachian Project, and a colleague, who happened to be a part-time Southern Baptist minister with literary interests, recommended I read a book called *Brother to a Dragonfly* by Will D.

Campbell, a memoir of Campbell's involvement with the civil rights movement. The book uses the first line of "Kingfishers" as its epigraph. Rev. Will's book was the first book I'd read that illuminated the complex connections of race and religion in the South and so clearly spoke to my own experience. Somehow, hiding behind the hatred or indifference that seems to surround us, there is a love that binds us all. That's what I took away from Campbell's moving book, and that is similar to what I take from this moving, spontaneous poem from Hopkins.

The poem is about the world and the terms upon which the human is invited to apprehend it. Here we have, apparently, a common necessity in Hopkins' time, commonly valued by individuals and communities. By imagining the sound of a stone tumbling down it, Hopkins turns the well into a musical instrument like an organ pipe or a flute. The tolling and telling from the well is followed by ringing bells as they send their sound over the countryside. Such images separated from their painterly effects make me think in more literal terms of what happens when space houses sound. That is a basic definition of music, of course. And somewhere above this scene, we can imagine a kingfisher chittering as it flies and a dragonfly bobbing in the air. Yet for all of the physical detail presented, the poem's perceptions are of the ethereal.

Hopkins must have known something about acoustics and vibration and resonance; certainly these properties of sound are embodied features of the poem—through the imagery and language and through the poem's main assertion. This mastery of sound, heard in language but tuned to the sounds heard in the world, is a key attribute of many of Hopkins' poems. "As Kingfishers Catch Fire" is a poem that needs to be read aloud—hearing it is more vital than reading it. I confess: reading it is a challenge! Yes, Hopkins observes detail, but in the detail, he glimpses a whole that cannot be reduced, and therefore what this poem is "saying" is multi-layered.

Many poems infer or even enact some form of reconciliation. A division is repaired. As Emerson says in his essay from 1844, "The Poet": "The poet re-attaches things to nature and the Whole." In this poem, however, Hopkins needs not bother with re-attaching because he recognizes the fundamental attachment that exists already: a fundamental attachment that, according to Hopkins, defines us. This gets to his concept of what he calls elsewhere "inscape." The inward beingness of nature and the inward beingness of the elements of nature, from the weather to kingfishers and dragonflies, from what can be seen to what can be heard, is the source of Hopkins' aesthetics. His vision associates the sacred with the natural—to declare that beauty, when properly perceived, is holy because it is true.

This is a poem about nature and language and is an effort to see the world as it is and our effort to articulate it. By doing so, we understand our place. Hopkins writes as if reading the world requires knowledge of a special language, suggesting that the world is unreadable yet revelatory, and thus the language of poetry must be heightened, infused, and conjoined. That is what we get from this wild Italian sonnet.

It's also worth noting that everything in this poem—every element of the world Hopkins observes and perceives—is vibrantly alive and vibrantly so. Many of Hopkins' poems, including this one, are rightly described as ecstatic. Yet for all of the ecstasy of this poem, it also follows formal conventions. The octave concerns itself with physical reality whereas the sestet brings the energy found in the physical realm to the interior, to the metaphysical, and to the spiritual.

As with most Hopkins' poems, our attention is captured by his wholly original use of language. The poem comprises just two sentences, neither of which would work in prose or ordinary speech. This is the language of exaltation; the formal features of the poem squeeze the language into lines, but that only intensifies the language. Hopkins enlivens the language through the meter and the rhyme but also through syntax and arresting diction. I think Hopkins is able to manage his wildness with the most powerful part of speech—his use of verbs. Consider the verbs in this poem and how Hopkins pairs them: catch/draw, ring/tells, finds/fling, does/deals, dwells/Selves, speaks/spells, crying, do/is, came. These are just the verbs from the octave—a lot of action packed into one sentence. Isolating them, we see all of the internal rhyme in the poem, suggesting that the poem's music is woven throughout and that the conventional form is used as a means to house transcendent sound. But these verbs also demonstrate how Hopkins sees the world: everything is animated, and the liveliness of all things begins in an interior state that must express itself outwardly, as if all creation sings out of itself to the Creator.

The sestet, notably, has far fewer verbs: "say," "justices" (a wonderful coinage), "Keeps," "keeps," "acts," "is," "plays." If the verbs of the octave point to the character of the natural world, then the verbs of the sestet point to the character of a human being—how we ought to be in the world. If we rightly observe creation and discover its inscape, then we may rightly see and properly be ourselves.

It's also true that many of the verbs Hopkins uses in this poem have multiple meanings or shades of meaning. Do kingfishers catch fire in the sense of combusting or in the sense of capturing? Do dragonflies draw flame in the sense of attracting or in the sense of rendering? Perhaps Hopkins wants his reader to experience all shades of meaning at once. Such verbs convey outward action and inward character, a blend of doing and being. To dwell, to add another example, can mean to reside and to inhabit, again a blend of an outward and an inward reality. This blended or mixed character of all living things is indeed what the poem is about. Thus Hopkins uses language—grammar!—to enact through poetic expression what he observes in the world. According to Hopkins' delightful journal entries, this was his vision all along: every feature of the world is alive and its distinct self but also seamlessly part of the whole.

I also appreciate that this poem is not about the poet or the poet's particular experience. It's a poem about the world though it is also found in the world, right in front of us. The poem's music invites us to memorize it and thereby belong with it. Hearing the poem makes us want to say what it says along with it, feeling it and absorbing it as we go.

It is worth noting that most of the key words in this poem are Anglo-Saxon in origin. This is not an original recognition, of course. Many readers have observed Hopkins' interest in the hard sounds and textures of Anglo-Saxon diction as well as his affection for local dialect and vernacular. Draw, dwell, and self (selves), for example, originate in Old English, a language that was tactile in its sound and also reflected more directly our physical contact with the world—when we plowed fields behind horses. Old English and our modern words that come from Anglo-Saxon origins are bodily and physical as opposed to being cerebral. Yet we also know Hopkins was surrounded by Latin—he taught Latin to his pupils, and as a priest, he would have heard the Catholic Mass in Latin, a language associated with the mind. I'm not sure if there is anything substantive to take from such an observation. Perhaps the language we have for the world and the living things in it—and the language we have for our place in the world—is simply stickier, reflecting the possibility that we live in the world by doing and being attached to it, and that is the language this poem gives us to hear. This is a poem of belonging and a celebration of that fact: a poem that reminds us of how we are and where we are. So be it.

Langston Hughes
1901–1967

Best known for: "Montage of a Dream Deferred,"
"The Weary Blues", "Harlem"

A key figure of the Harlem Renaissance, Langston Hughes was a Missouri-born poet who made his name while living in New York City. He was an innovator of jazz poetry, and incorporated syncopation and repetition into traditional verse forms thus mirroring the improvisational nature of jazz and blues music. But his innovation was on behalf of the people who "intend to express our individual dark-skinned selves without fear or shame." He said that his poetry was about the:

"workers, roustabouts, and singers, and job hunters on Lenox Avenue in New York, or Seventh Street in Washington or South State in Chicago—people up today and down tomorrow, working this week and fired the next, beaten and baffled, but determined not to be wholly beaten, buying furniture on the installment plan, filling the house with roomers to help pay the rent, hoping to get a new suit for Easter—and pawning that suit before the Fourth of July."

As much as any poet in this collection, Hughes was the voice of his own people. As David Littlejohn wrote, "By molding his verse always on the sounds of Negro talk, the rhythms of Negro music, by retaining his own keen honesty and directness, his poetic sense and ironic intelligence, he maintained through four decades a readable newness distinctly his own."

{poem}
The Negro Speaks of Rivers

I've known rivers:
I've known rivers ancient as the world and older than
  the flow of human blood in human veins.

My soul has grown deep like the rivers.

I bathed in the Euphrates when dawns were young.
I built my hut near the Congo and it lulled me to sleep.
I looked upon the Nile and raised the pyramids above it.
I heard the singing of the Mississippi when Abe Lincoln
  went down to New Orleans, and I've seen its muddy
  bosom turn all golden in the sunset.

I've known rivers:
Ancient, dusky rivers.

My soul has grown deep like the rivers.

{reflection}

The Slow Accretion of Experience

by Christine Perrin

Langston Hughes was born in 1902 in Joplin, Missouri. He began writing poetry in Illinois but lived in a variety of places, including Mexico. He was greatly influenced by Walt Whitman so much so that, when he took a steamer across the Atlantic, he threw all his other books overboard. His varied work experience and travels, as well as his exposure to jazz and the blues, show up in his work in all sorts of ways. His contribution to the Harlem Renaissance was substantial, and the voice he used in his work did not distinguish between his own experience and the common experience of African Americans. He wrote in almost every literary genre available and widely promoted other African American artists of all kinds. He sought to bring the rhythms and sensibility of jazz into his mostly open-verse poetry. The laughter, language, suffering, excellence, boasts, and embarrassments of African American culture were all explored in his work—he pursued transparency and reality in his portraits. Zora Neale Hurston, a collaborator of his, voiced their common disposition to America in this period this way: "Sometimes, I feel discriminated against, but it does not make me angry. It merely astonishes me. How can any deny themselves the pleasure of my company?"

"The Negro Speaks of Rivers" is an essential poem in Hughes' collection despite the fact that he wrote it when he was just eighteen years old. In various recitations of the poem, he explained how he wrote it when traveling by train to visit his father in Mexico and passed over the Mississippi River, which flows through ten states. He began to think about what this river meant to his people. His grandmother, who raised him until age thirteen, had described to him what a terrible thing it was to be sold on the Mississippi as a slave. Hughes knew that Abraham Lincoln had seen the slave trade on the river when he was a young man, never forgot it, and went on to sign the Emancipation Proclamation. As Hughes contemplated the muddy river turning golden at sunset, he took out a letter from his father and wrote this poem on the back of it.

A beautiful poem to recite, it borrows the long psalmic rhythms of Walt Whitman's poetry. The repetitions and stanza breaks serve as ruminative and cumulative space: a two-lined stanza, one-lined stanza, four-lined stanza, two-lined stanza, one-lined stanza. Note the accordion-like expansion accruing force, wisdom, and depth. Sometimes these sections can serve as a memory device. The phrase "I've known rivers" is repeated three times throughout and serves the sensation of gathered time and action. The phrase "my soul has grown deep like the rivers" functions like a bookend in line three and in line ten (the last).

This poem is a classic example of Hughes' act of claiming the voice of his people and of speaking for African American peoples throughout history and across vast geography—by claiming the rivers that flowed through those places: Euphrates, Congo, Nile, Mississippi. First, he binds the soul and heritage of this expansive community to the Euphrates that is pre-racial and geographically far from Africa—considered the location of the Garden of Eden and the genesis of human civilization. At the same time that he identifies with the unity of people of color in every country and every age, he links to a mystical geography that is not identified with blackness or whiteness. Thus he lays claim to an accumulated wisdom as profound and deep as the rivers of civilization and the beginning of time. The other rivers (Congo and Nile) link directly to slavery over extensive time and wide location, and the Mississippi registers the very recent past of American slave history. He invokes this without ever saying the word "slavery" and imbeds the sensation of depth, accumulation, time, gathering force, and fluency in the formal choices of the poem.

He uses a simple repetitive syntax—"I bathed," "I built," "I looked upon," "I heard"—to precede the mention of these places and his identification with his brothers and sisters who lived lives near these rivers. Notice how the anaphora creates the sensation of mounting and collective experience. There are glimpses of oppression and suffering that happened in these places, such as when the speaker mentions having "raised the pyramids" above the Nile. There's the historical memory of Abe Lincoln encountering the persecution on the Mississippi as a young man. But there is also a mysterious, even proud, claim that this suffering has produced a depth of soul akin to that of rivers and their long presence. This profound and ancient knowledge of rivers has produced beauty and wisdom that cannot be taken away or threatened by the misery that accompanied the knowledge-gaining process.

Throughout the poem, the reader feels the pull and flow of the river water in the lines—the slow accretion of experience. We encounter a layering effect achieved by the repetition and the rhythms. The pauses are essential to recitation, but there are also returns everywhere. Note the "I've," "my," and "I" markers that exist at the beginnings of lines throughout. The word "river" is repeated six times. Like Whitman, Hughes includes some very long lines that don't fit on the page. When a line doesn't fit on a standard page, the formatting rules for a lyric poem require it to be indented, and sometimes this is hard to distinguish from an open verse form that has chosen indention. This poem has ten lines in total—five stanzas and eight sentences. The potential arrestors or retarders of movement are worth pondering both in relation to the meaning and according to the emphasis you choose. The stanza breaks combined with periods or ends of sentences, in particular, direct this but so also do the long vowels ("known," "older," "soul," "grown," etc.) and some of the line breaks. Most of the lines are self-contained with a period at the end of each. This requires us to slow down and stop. At the same time, the repetition of key phrases and syntactical units ("I've known," "My soul," "I bathed," "I built," "I looked," "I heard") makes us move sequentially without really moving—we learn and grow but we dwell and collect at the same time. Most of the lines are long with the short lines layered liturgically on top of the line that follows them, contributing to the sensation mentioned earlier of gathered time and action. Rivers have a long history of fertility and life-sustenance; water remembers where it has been and shapes the human and geologic reality with its powerful flow. At once, the poem formally creates that power, momentum, and place-holding with these devices of repetition combined with movement.

Tone is one of the most essential elements to consider when reciting a poem. To decide what the tone of a poem is, you have to be a careful reader—sifting and synthesizing many factors. Think about what happens when you say hello to someone who delights you, versus hello to someone you don't know, or versus hello when you are feeling sullen. The same words get repeated in very different variations. One of the most virtuous, mysterious, and even enchanting aspects of this poem is its tone of assurance. The declarative sentences are combined with the device of anaphora—syntactical repetition— thus while the declaration is firm and confident, it is also serene and stable. The simplicity of the diction and eloquence add to the sensation of strength and fullness—not alarm or dispute. Ending with a return to a refrain first mentioned in line three ("My soul has grown deep …") also gives the perception of having survived such troubles in the bosom of the golden rivers—singing, fluent, full-bodied, and flowing still through time, place, and human ingenuity.

Elizabeth Jennings
1926–2001

Best known for: A Way of Looking,
"A Bird in the House"

English poet Elizabeth Jennings was born in Boston, Lincolnshire. After moving to Oxford when she was six years old, she lived there for the rest of her life, attending St. Anne's College and becoming a writer. The only female member of a group of English formal writers called "The Movement," Jennings was known for her adherence to traditional poetic forms, particularly the sonnet. The Movement, which also included Philip Larkin and Kingsley Amis, was dedicated to elevating the cultural supremacy of English formalism over what they saw as the encroaching threat of a more global—and particularly American—modernism. These poets were alarmed by the decreasing political and cultural prominence of England in world affairs, so they attempted to spearhead a return to the conventions of long-established English poetics—including pastoral imagery, traditional forms, and a celebration of a typically "English" way of life. At the same time that Jennings, a devout Roman Catholic, was advancing the conservative cause of the Movement through penning traditional poetry, she was also combating personal demons. Known as the "bag lady of the sonnet," Jennings, desperately poor, battled bouts of severe mental illness, sometimes being admitted to psychiatric hospitals. The complex relationship between Jennings' conventional style, deep faith, and troubled inner life resulted in a poetic canon of manifold subtlety and tenderness. The apparently simple formal elements of her poetry juxtapose the complexity of the dark grace she explored throughout her body of work. In 1992, Jennings was honored by Queen Elizabeth as a CBE (Commander of the Order of the British Empire) for her many achievements as a poet. Jennings died in 2001 in a nursing home in Oxford.

{poem}
Act of the Imagination

Surely an Act of the Imagination
Helps more than one of Faith
When a doubt brushes us. We need strong passion
To summon miracles. Life after death,

Bread turning into flesh and blood from wine,
I need to cast around
And find an image for the most divine
Concepts. My mind must move on holy ground,

And then the hardest creed – the rising from
Death when Christ indeed
Bled finally – ideas cannot come
As barren notions. Yes, I always need

Herbert's sonnet 'Prayer' say, or that great
Giotto painting for
My heart to leap to God. I want to meet
Him in my own poems, God as metaphor

And rising up. I watch a lucid sky
And see a silver cloud
And Christ's behind it; this is part of faith,

Hear the Great Hours sung and let faith be loud
With the best imagining we have.
This is how I approach
My God-made-Man. Thus I learn to love
And yes, like Thomas, know Christ through a touch.

{reflection}

The Language of the Heart
by Ian Andrews

In "Act of the Imagination," Elizabeth Jennings joins a long tradition of poets who succeed in demonstrating the idea *about* which they are writing *as* they write about it. Over six quatrains, Jennings meditates on the powerful ability of artistic expression to embody, apply, and verify faith. In so doing, she uses her own art to do this very thing— defending the place of art in worship and expressing not only the artist's desire to meet God in their own art but also their responsibility to seek Him there.

Beyond the ABAB rhyme scheme, which is consistent throughout (despite the fact that some of the rhymes are sight rhymes rather than sound rhymes), Jennings eschews metrical structure. While the second line of each quatrain consists in each case of three iambic feet, the other three lines evince no consistent number of stresses or even syllables. This lack of rigidity allows Jennings to adopt a conversational tone, exploring the corners of her central thought in sentences of disparate length. The line breaks themselves not only produce rhyme but also nearly constant enjambment, inviting the reader to linger on important words that they may otherwise have passed over. A sterling example comes in the first stanza where Jennings drapes the following sentence over the break between the third and fourth lines: "We need strong passion/To summon miracles." Since the sentence straddles the line break, our eye rests a beat longer on the final word of line three, "passion," before jumping down to finish the sentence. This encourages the reader to chew on the first half of the statement in the absence of the following phrase: "We need strong passion." Firstly this statement proves to be an apt summary of Jennings' defense of the place of art in one's faith journey. It also, however, conjures religious imagery aplenty, calling to mind the Passion in all its numerous depictions in paint and stone as well as print.

Given the frequent use of enjambment and the relative lack of structure, memorizing this poem demands a deep understanding of Jennings's imagery and a firm grasp of her theme—as many of the helpful metrical and structural aids to memorization are absent.

Jennings begins by making a bold statement: "Surely an Act of the Imagination/Helps more than one of Faith/when a doubt brushes us." This line first identifies the universal target of this poem: those afflicted by doubt—the presence of which makes faith itself a miracle. Jennings further asserts that this miracle is only possible in the grip of strong passions equal to the task of overcoming the natural limitations of our belief. Such passions, according to Jennings, are conjured by acts of the imagination. Another significant use of enjambment in the poem comes in the last line of the first stanza, where Jennings calls out the ultimate example of a "divine [c]oncept" that the human mind cannot grasp without miraculous help—Resurrection.

She goes on, in the second stanza, to further define her own limitations, and, by extension, those of her readers as ones connected
intimately with our worldly frames—we finite creatures cannot step
wholly into the divine as faith would have us do. We must instead,
see, feel, hear, and touch that in which we are asked to believe. We
must have bread to chew and wine to drink or else the spiritual flesh
and blood are only ideas. We must have an image of the concept to
grasp it with our minds. The "ground" she refers to in the final line of
the second stanza is "holy," but it is also "ground." In considering "the
most divine/Concepts," Jennings and her reader need those concepts
to be expressed in an earthly, or even earthy, way.

The third stanza contains the thematic center of the poem, what
Jennings calls "the hardest creed"—Christ's death and resurrection,
which is ultimate proof of the poet's assertion that "ideas cannot
come/As barren notions." Christ did not save the world as he created
it: with a word. He saved it bodily, by bleeding physically and rising
physically from the grave. Belief in such an earth-shattering, unnatural series of events must be likewise incarnated—brought home to
our human hearts in human fashion.

Here at the turn of the poem, Jennings's tone shifts ever so slightly. Whereas the "surely" of the first line betrays the poet's desire to
reassure herself and her reader that their doubts and their need for
help in conquering them are common and natural, the "Yes, I always
need ..." and the references that follow are triumphant, loving, and
exuberant as the poet's heart "leap[s] to God." This shift comes directly after Jennings points out that God himself carried out the very

metaphor she writes about in the Incarnation—Jesus took on created flesh, stepping into an act of the imagination to ratify and establish our faith. With such vindication on the side of the doubter, the poet is now free to exult in the inspiration and spiritual edification that works of art can offer.

Jennings then marshals two examples—Herbert's sonnet, "Prayer" and an unnamed Giotto painting. Fittingly both are intended to perform the very office she ascribes to "acts of the imagination." A quick reading of Herbert's sonnet 'Prayer' reveals a torrent of metaphors describing prayer, building to the final comforting assertion that prayer is "something understood." Each metaphor makes concrete something that is, as anyone who has ever prayed knows well, often scattered and distracted. Herbert's art gives both form and substance to his praises. Jennings doesn't mention a particular painting, but Giotto's large body of spiritual works reflect the same impulse Jennings lauds: to encourage and empower the viewer to commune with the Creator.

Her desire, however, does not stop at meeting God in the works of others; she dares to hope that she will meet Him in pursuit of her own craft as well: "God as metaphor,/And rising up." Here in the fifth stanza, she begins a stirring apology for the Christian artist's burden and calling: to "watch a lucid sky/And see a silver cloud/And Christ's behind it." In such natural phenomena, the artist is not only tasked with seeing the Creator but also with proclaiming Him the great artist, lending all His creation tongues with which to sing His praises. If He, in His holy making, chose to clothe ideas in beauty and form, then those who do likewise do so in imitation of their Creator.

"[L]et faith be loud/With the best imagining we have."

Jennings yearns, as do we all, for a sensory, earthy experience with transcendental ideas. She is all too familiar with the brushing fingertips of doubt, ever present in the most powerful and pivotal concepts, and she knows faith cannot be grasped but must instead be evoked. And the Christ she seeks looks on her need with kindness. He doesn't demand that she be something other than what she is—a creature. Instead He speaks to her in a language that her heart can hear—that of beauty powerful enough to inspire and to sustain her faith as well as all acts of the imagination.

Such imaginings as this one can be seen and heard and loved. And in such a fashion, all we doubting Thomases may be blessed to learn, as Jennings has, to love and "to know Christ through a touch."

Nine More Poems from the Romantic Era Worth Memorizing

This volume includes a handful of poems from the Romantics, including poems by Shelley, Keats, and Wordsworth, but the period was rich with highly memorizable poems. In fact, for all its political interests, the Romantic era is most defined by craftsmen and women pursuing beauty—and it shows in the lines they produced. Here are a few worth adding to your reportoire:

"The Tyger" by William Blake

"She Walks in Beauty" by Lord Byron (George Gordon)

"To Autumn" by John Keats

"Kubla Kahn" by Samuel Taylor Coleridge

"Huge Vapours Brood above the Clifted Shore" by Charlotte Smith

"The Hackney Coachman: Or the Way to Get a Good Fare"
by Hannah More

"My Heart Leaps Up" by William Wordsworth

"The Skylark" by John Clare

"A Red, Red Rose" by Robert Burns

To learn more about Romanticism, turn to page 543 of Edward Hirsch's A Poet's Glossary.

John Keats
1795–1821

*Best known for: "Ode on a Grecian Urn,"
"Ode to a Nightingale," "To Autumn"*

One of the great Romantic poets, John Keats was the eldest of four children. At the age of eight, he was enrolled in John Clarke boarding school where he developed a lifelong fascination with history and classics. Alas, his father, a stable keeper at the Swan and Hoop Inn, was trampled to death by a horse when young John was eight years old, and his mother, who fared poorly as a widow, died of tuberculosis when he was fourteen. His parents' deaths—particularly his father's—profoundly influenced him both as an individual and as a poet. Keats lived a very short life, but his poetry indicates a ripe understanding of the rich continuum of the human condition, both life and death, suffering and joy—legacies from his disrupted childhood. Keats became an apothecary by trade, but his real love was literature. His boarding school friend and mentor, Cowden Clarke, connected young Keats to publisher Leigh Hunt, who had an eye for young talent. Keats, then twenty, began publishing poetry and developed relationships with Wordsworth, Shelley, and other Romantic poets. Driven by his deep love for his craft, Keats dedicated himself to the perfection of the art, and he became known for elegant formal technique, vivid idealized descriptions of the natural world, profound philosophical contemplations, and integration of classical legends. Although acclaimed within his own literary community, his poetry was largely ignored or condemned by established critics of his day. It was only after his death that his genius was recognized by the wider community, and his reputation grew steadily until he was the most beloved of all English poets by the end of the nineteenth century. Keats died slowly and painfully at age twenty-five from tuberculosis, which he contracted on a walking tour while gathering material for his work.

{poem}
Bright Star

Bright star, would I were stedfast as thou art—
        Not in lone splendour hung aloft the night
And watching, with eternal lids apart,
        Like nature's patient, sleepless Eremite,
The moving waters at their priestlike task
        Of pure ablution round earth's human shores,
Or gazing on the new soft-fallen mask
        Of snow upon the mountains and the moors—
No—yet still stedfast, still unchangeable,
        Pillow'd upon my fair love's ripening breast,
To feel for ever its soft fall and swell,
        Awake for ever in a sweet unrest,
Still, still to hear her tender-taken breath,
And so live ever—or else swoon to death.

{reflection}
The Search for Real Presence
by Ian Andrews

To read Keats well, one must apprehend the tragedy that indelibly marked his short life. Young John lost both parents by the age of fourteen after which he and his two brothers were raised by his grandmother. The family finances, however, were taken over by two legal guardians his mother appointed before her death, neither of whom informed the boys of their bequests: two sums of money totaling in the neighborhood of £8,800 (£550,000 in modern terms). Consequently all three boys struggled financially all their lives, straying in and out of crippling debt and poor living conditions. All three died of tuberculosis relatively young, John himself at the age of twenty-five.

Despite the fact that he had been writing for less than a decade and publishing for only four years by the time of his death, Keats produced a remarkable body of work consisting of both poetry and a large number of letters. It is partially due to this correspondence that the extent of Keats' genius is apparent: his philosophy and theory of poetry are as robust a contribution to literary romanticism as his poetic works themselves.

Keats was intensely introspective, writing as often about himself and his own perception of his thinking as he did about the world around him. It is from this well of introspection that "Bright Star" springs.

"Bright Star" is a Shakespearean sonnet. The traditional form of a sonnet, a Petrarchan sonnet, was perfected in the Renaissance and consists of an octave, (eight rhyming lines) followed by a sestet (six rhyming lines). The change in rhyme scheme between the first eight lines and the second six lines of a Petrachan sonnet denotes a shift in thought—while the first eight lines pose a problem, the final six suggest a solution.

During the Elizabethan era, English poets began to write a particular variation on the Petrarchan sonnet that was perfected by Shakespeare and bears his name to this day. In a Shakespearean sonnet, the poet constructs three quatrains (each four rhyming lines) followed by a final couplet (two rhyming lines). While the ideas in a Petrarchan sonnet hinge in the middle of the poem during the transition between octave and sestet, the turn in a Shakespearean sonnet happens at the final moment during the couplet. This has the effect of heightening tension—and making the resolution pithy and impactful.

In "Bright Star," however, Keats seems to have twinned the sonnet forms—he employs the Shakespearean rhyme scheme but his ideas follow the Petrarchan conceptual structure. We see three quatrains, rhyming ABAB CDCD and EFEF followed by a couplet, rhyming GG. The turn of the poem, however, takes place at the beginning of the ninth line of the poem. As you memorize, it will be helpful to take this poem first in four parts, taking quatrains and couplet in turn—and again in two conceptual chunks, conceiving of the first two quatrains as building up to a climactic moment of turning followed by the final quatrain and couplet offering the poet's ultimate idea.

Keats opens his poem with an **apostrophe**: a literary device that directly addresses an inanimate object. In this case, a star. He wastes no time in making the star, and his reader, aware of his yearning: to be "stedfast" as the star is steadfast. The use of this word to describe both the star and his own desired state suggests two meanings—firstly a desire to be eternal or immortal and secondly a desire to be emotionally stable or intellectually firm. The poet searches both his human frame and his mind and heart and finds both to be fleeting and transient. In the case of his heart, this carries with it a sense of emotional inconstancy that will become even more pronounced during the third quatrain.

Beginning in the second line, Keats sharpens the idea of steadfastness by contrasting his desire with a long list of things about the star's life that he does not in fact want to emulate. He does not want to be "lone" or to be merely a spectator to the happenings of the world. Particularly interesting in this regard is his personification of the star embodied in the word "Eremite": a Christian ascetic or hermit. Keats wants to be eternal but not eternally solitary like the star or like a hermit, no matter how pure their respective lives may be.

These two entities, the star and the hermit, carry with them different kinds of purity. For the true proponent of Romanticism, intense human emotion, especially that caused by an experience with the sublimity of nature's beauty, is the wellspring of truth and personal identity. So the star, being a part of nature and a witness to its movement—the "priestlike ablution" of the oceans, the purity of new fallen snow on the mountains and moors—evokes the deepest emotional response. Describing the star further as a hermit, however, Keats compounds the purity of nature with spiritual purity before summarily rejecting both in favor of an as yet unexplained aspect of the steadfastness he seeks but cannot seem to grasp.

In the ninth line, the beginning of the third quatrain, he signals to his reader that he's about to clarify by saying "No—yet still stedfast, still unchangeable": This affirms his rejection of the pure and lonely life of the Eremite star while re-invoking the single word he has chosen to represent his yearning.

What follows is a description utterly opposed to the austere and cold life of the first two quatrains. We see the poet "[p]illow'd upon [his] fair love's ripening breast" where the "soft fall and swell" of her breathing twines rest and the continual wakefulness of a living thing into one perfect awareness of self and other. Keats longs for something more than simple immortality—not for an eternity alone but an eternity of ultimate presence and relationship. The final line of the third quatrain, however, points out the central paradox and conflict of the poem. In contrasting the sweetness of repose with "unrest," which implies both the physical unrest of wakefulness and the emotional and spiritual unrest he has been yearning to defeat all along, Keats demonstrates a painful awareness of the human condition. We are eternal souls pent up in prisons of flesh. Our deepest yearnings, those that are fundamental to our spiritual being, cannot be slaked in the flesh no matter how deeply we wish to see, touch, and hold them.

He initiates the final couplet with a repetitive "[s]till, still." A careful reader will notice, especially as one plays with emphases while reading aloud or reciting, that the first "[s]till" functions as a synonym for "yet" as well as a somewhat tired admonition to the soul to cease the spiritual struggle in favor of earthly rest: a total experience of love, untroubled by intellectual examinations, doubts, or fears.

> *Still, still to hear her tender-taken breath,*
> *And so live ever—or else swoon to death.*

To paraphrase: "Yet, quiet—utterly focused—on the steady rise and fall of her breathing forever. And if I can't be such a man, one steadfast enough to bend all my faculties on this one experience of pure, natural peace, I'd rather die." One senses the poet's distaste for the abstractions that his mind constantly encourages—why must he always think about love instead of merely loving? Why can he not be fully embroiled in his passion yet remain fully intellectually aware of it? The tragic truth is that mankind is ever faced with his own inability to be truly present in his mind and heart, to fully engage with the world around him. One cannot be passionate and yet unmoved. One cannot separate body and soul this side of eternity.

Though Keats himself may have found little peace, his poem remains a beautiful reminder of the need all hold within them: though this earth is not our home, we are not long for it. And true presence of mind, heart, and body may yet be our lot.

Jane Kenyon
1947–1995

Best known for: "Let Evening Come"
"Having it Out with Melancholy"

Originally from Michigan where she attended college at the University of Michigan in Ann Arbor, Jane Kenyon died in New Hampshire where she lived with her husband, Donald Hall, at Eagle Pond Farm. Together they made up one of the most prodigious literary couples in American history. Although Hall (her teacher once upon a time) is more widely read today, Kenyon was his equal in many ways. She served as the poet laureate to New Hampshire, won the PEN/Volkner award, and produced two of the most beloved poems of the twentieth century in "Let Evening Comes," which you find here, and "Having it Out with Melancholy." At the time of her death from leukemia in 1995, she was at work on her final collection, *Otherwise: New and Selected Poems.* Her other collections include *Constance* (1993), *Let Evening Come* (1990), *The Boat of Quiet Hours* (1986), and *From Room to Room* (1978). Today she is remembered as a "Keastsian poet," as Gary Roberts called her in *Contemporary Women Poets,* "who attempts to redeem morbidity with a peculiar kind of gusto, one which seeks a quiet annihilation of self-identity through identification with benign things."

{poem}

Let Evening Come

Let the light of late afternoon
shine through chinks in the barn, moving
up the bales as the sun moves down.

Let the cricket take up chafing
as a woman takes up her needles
and her yarn. Let evening come.

Let dew collect on the hoe abandoned
in long grass. Let the stars appear
and the moon disclose her silver horn.

Let the fox go back to its sandy den.
Let the wind die down. Let the shed
go black inside. Let evening come.

To the bottle in the ditch, to the scoop
in the oats, to air in the lung
let evening come.

Let it come, as it will, and don't
be afraid. God does not leave us
comfortless, so let evening come.

{reflection}
An Unnegotiable Demand
by David Kern

When Jane Kenyon died of leukemia in April of 1995 at the age of forty-seven, she had accomplished what most poets only dream of. Equally popular among the reading public and her poet-colleagues, she was genuinely successful. She inspired the lay reader because she could speak to—and sometimes for—them, and she inspired other poets because she was fearless in her precision and uniquely capable of hearing the music in language. As Wendell Berry once wrote, "She had a virtually faultless ear."

A decade after her death, Berry and many other admirers contributed to a collection of remembrances of her life and work called *Simply Lasting: Writers on Jane Kenyon*. Collectively the entries in this compendium offer a thoughtful ode to Kenyon's place in the canon of American poets: Their loving, awe-filled reflections on her capabilities suggest that she belongs at the top of any such list and for many of the same reasons that "Let Evening Come" shows up in the anthology you are reading now.

The essays found in *Simply Lasting* suggest that the quotidian images and unadorned vocabulary Kenyon employed in her poems offer readers a sense of truth, goodness, and beauty more profoundly than most other poets could ever hope to reveal, no matter how gilded their poems. She was a great poet not because she could do shock and awe, but because she could make the simplest of things seem grand, the most unassuming of phrases seem lofty. This is why she remains popular today, a decade and a half after her death: because she produced poems that are stately without being imposing. In short, she produced dignified poems.

"Let Evening Come" is such a poem (and is worth memorizing) because it does so much more than it seems to be doing. This is true of many great poems although not all, but it's a particularly necessary characteristic when discussing memorization. If we're going to spend a lot of time with a poem, the poem should give us something to feast on—and poems that surprise at their depth are particularly delightful hosts.

Here we have a poem that is about death, but also courage; that is hopeful, but realistic; that has the tone of Kipling's famous poem, "If," but avoids the sentimentality Kipling's treads so near. "Let Evening Come" makes no promises, and yet contemplative readers might feel as if they've been given new life as they spend time with it. Kenyan's poem is at once assertive and reassuring, sanguine and melancholy. It's a hopeful poem about darkness. And she manages to accomplish this because her tone is so deliberately full of light. She says things to the deepest parts of our souls that feel, at first, as simple as a sophisticated nursery rhyme but that allow light to shine on the "chinks" of our cynicism and despair. This is why Berry wrote that "her voice always carries the tremor of feeling disciplined by art. This is what over and over again enabled her to take the risk of plainness, or of apparent plainness."

Consider, for example, the pace of these eighteen lines. Like many pastoral poems, "Let Evening Come" sets out leisurely. The first line, with its alliteration, slows the reader down (try reading "let the light of late afternoon" quickly without tripping up) before the poem has even begun while lines two and three suggest objects moving in opposite directions. More precisely, Kenyon describes the light of the sun moving up the bales of hay in the barn while the sun itself descends beyond the horizon. As the sun disappears, its rays enlighten the hay that crosses its path. So, on the one hand, she is slowing the reader down, and on the other hand, she is pursuing movement. That paradox shows up throughout the poem. The end-stopped lines that conclude stanzas two and four, for example, cause the reader to stop and contemplate the newly completed thought, but they also signal a transition in the poem to a further exploration of the central idea. In this, they are ideal markers for the reader who is looking to memorize this poem.

Meanwhile the first line offers the first of twelve imperative statements nestled throughout the poem, all of which begin with the phrase "[l]et the." "Let the line shine," she says. "Let the crickets take up chafing." "Let dew collect." "Let evening come." And the magic of the poem is found in the way this imperative demand merges with the paradoxical ideas of freedom and obstruction. Let the light shine through, she says, but also let it leave. Let the light shine through, but also let the stars appear—let night fall. Let the sun shine through, but also let the shed go black—and all of this through the ironically imperative nature of the case she's making for the reader. Thus the poem opens with the ostensibly hopeful image of the bright-shining sun that offers solace, but it argues that the reader must ultimately not cling to that brightness too tightly.

Then in the final two stanzas, the pace picks up. With a series of short phrases marked by short (Germanic) words, Kenyon briskly whisks us to the concluding tercet: "To the bottle in the ditch, to the scoop/in the oats, to the air in the lung/let evening come." To this point, the images have been idyllic, made up of pleasant familiar natural scenes, and the phrasing of the lines has been bucolic. But here, in the penultimate stanza, Kenyon races through the images as if turning her attention to a winter's day when the sun proceeds beyond the horizon so quickly that late afternoon hardly has a chance to appear.

Finally in the last stanza, she brings it all together. "[D]on't/be afraid," she implores. "God does not leave us/comfortless, so let evening come." Evening will come for one and all; it will most certainly come, and when it comes, it will seem as if it has a mind of its own, a will of its own. It will arrive, and the day will feel like it was hardly ever here. But take courage, she says; have faith. Do not obscure your capacity to endure; do not bury your belief in the Almighty. Let the light of the afternoon shine through.

Wendell Berry wrote in *Simply Lasting* that Kenyon's work "makes an unnegotiable demand upon a reader. It doesn't demand great intellect or learning or even sympathy. It demands quiet." Well, memorizing a poem is one of the purest ways to embody the experience of being quiet with a poem because it allows the music of a poem to emerge over time in an unobtrusive fashion. "Let Evening Come" may seem plain—to use Berry's term—but it's that plainness that makes it so worth spending time with, for emerging from the simple surface are paradoxes that pave the way like constellations for a pioneer.

William Shakespeare
1564–1616

Best known for: Hamlet, Romeo and Juliet,
Much Ado About Nothing

William Shakespeare was arguably the greatest writer ever to wield a pen in the English language. He was born in 1564 in Stratford-upon-Avon in England, the son of prosperous middle class parents. At the age of eighteen, young William married Anne Hathaway with whom he had three children. Soon he began a successful career as an actor, playwright, and partner in a theater company called the Lord Chamberlain's Men. His plays were performed at London's famous Globe Theater to great renown. Over the course of two decades, Shakespeare wrote 38 plays, 154 sonnets, two long narrative poems, and various other poems. Best known for his plays, Shakespeare was equally adept in writing comedy, tragedy, and history. Wildly popular in his lifetime, Shakespeare's work appealed both to the masses and to the aristocracy. His theater company even performed before Queen Elizabeth and King James I. Shakespeare retired to his childhood home in Stratford-upon-Avon at the age of forty-nine where he died three years later. After his death, his contemporaries, recognizing his genius, collected his scattered works for posterity. Not much is known about Shakespeare's private life, but his mastery of the English language and the theatrical genre remains unparalleled. His skill as a wordsmith was prodigious; he invented dozens of words and phrases still in colloquial use today such as "be-all end-all," "barefaced," and "catch a cold." Translated into every major language, Shakespeare's plays continue to be performed more than the work of any other playwright in the history of the world. His collected works are outsold only by the Bible.

{poem}
Mark Antony's Funeral Oration from *Julius Caesar*

Friends, Romans, countrymen, lend me your ears;
I come to bury Caesar, not to praise him.
The evil that men do lives after them;
The good is oft interred with their bones;
So let it be with Caesar. The noble Brutus
Hath told you Caesar was ambitious:
If it were so, it was a grievous fault,
And grievously hath Caesar answer'd it.
Here, under leave of Brutus and the rest—
For Brutus is an honourable man;
So are they all, all honourable men—
Come I to speak in Caesar's funeral.
He was my friend, faithful and just to me:
But Brutus says he was ambitious;
And Brutus is an honourable man.
He hath brought many captives home to Rome
Whose ransoms did the general coffers fill:
Did this in Caesar seem ambitious?
When that the poor have cried, Caesar hath wept:
Ambition should be made of sterner stuff:
Yet Brutus says he was ambitious;
And Brutus is an honourable man.
You all did see that on the Lupercal
I thrice presented him a kingly crown,

Which he did thrice refuse: was this ambition?
Yet Brutus says he was ambitious;
And, sure, he is an honourable man.
I speak not to disprove what Brutus spoke,
But here I am to speak what I do know.
You all did love him once, not without cause:
What cause withholds you then, to mourn for him?
O judgment! thou art fled to brutish beasts,
And men have lost their reason. Bear with me;
My heart is in the coffin there with Caesar,
And I must pause till it come back to me.

{reflection}

The Ceremonial Rhetoric of a Political Mastermind
by Matthew Bianco

William Shakespeare needs no introduction—or at least he ought not need one. Perhaps he does. As more and more schools, colleges, and universities divest themselves of the playwright's rich works, fewer and fewer of us will know him or his plays. As the author of over thirty plays and 150 plus sonnets, he is one of the greatest literary minds, a truth evinced especially in "Mark Antony's Funeral Oration."

Both a poem and a work of rhetoric, this speech is found in Shakespeare's play, *Julius Caesar*, in which a group of conspirators, led by Brutus, have just assassinated the leader of Rome, Julius Caesar—a scene that ends, of course, with the famous, "Et tu, Brute?" Following that scene, Brutus delivers a speech to the nearby crowd of plebeians before agreeing to allow Mark Antony the opportunity to speak, too. Brutus speaks as a conspirator, explaining their actions to the crowd. Antony, a friend to Caesar and not a conspirator himself, speaks as a new friend to the conspirators and to lend his support to their cause—or so Brutus supposes.

Mark Antony's speech is an example of one of Shakespeare's most genius techniques: He often writes with a combination of prose and poetry. Sometimes, different characters speak in either prose or verse (sometimes the same character will speak in prose then in verse), and the manner of speaking communicates to the audience something about the particular character. In many of his plays, the upper class characters (the nobility or royalty) speak in verse, while commoners speak in prose. In some instances, the wise or the good characters speak in verse while the foolish, mad, or evil characters speak in prose. Tellingly in these two funeral speeches, Brutus speaks in prose while Mark Antony speaks in verse.

Why does Shakespeare do this? Both characters are nobility. Is one wise and the other foolish or mad? Is one good and the other evil? While Shakespeare's use of verse and prose suggests answers to these questions, it does not necessitate those conclusions. What it does leave us with, though, is a rhetorical poem (or poetic rhetoric) that is worth memorizing because of what it is and what it does (to the characters in the play). It is a poem, moreover, that is worth memorizing because of how brilliantly it demonstrates the genius of Shakespeare himself.

Mark Antony's funeral oration is a kind of classical rhetoric practiced by the Greeks and Romans through the early Church, the Medieval Age, and even into today. Classical rhetoric develops three forms based on the three kinds of questions humans are always asking and trying to answer. These three primary forms of rhetoric are judicial, deliberative, and ceremonial. Judicial rhetoric is used in the courts: speeches used to persuade a judge or jury to make a just decision regarding a defendant's behavior. Deliberative rhetoric is used in government: speeches used to persuade lawmakers to make honorable or expedient decisions regarding legislative questions. Ceremonial rhetoric is used in public events: speeches used to persuade crowds to esteem a person or persons praiseworthy or to censure them. A funeral oration is a public event at which ceremonial rhetoric would be practiced in order to remind the crowd why the dead should be praised or remembered.

Mark Antony's funeral oration is brilliant because it purports to be one of those kinds of rhetoric and not the other kinds while actually serving as all three. "Friends, Romans, countrymen, lend me your ears." These words necessarily address a public gathering, not a law court or a legislative body. He addresses the public at the death of their leader; it almost necessarily follows that he is about to give a funeral oration. He then says, "I come to bury Caesar, not to praise him." He is, in effect, telling the audience, "You think I am come to give a ceremonial address in praise of Caesar, but I am not. Instead, I am going to bury Caesar and tell you how we should judge Brutus instead." He shifts the focus of the speech in that single line.

This introduction is exactly the kind of exordium Cicero suggests should be used when addressing a hostile audience—which the Roman crowd, having just heard and agreed with Brutus's speech, now is. This exordium is a clarification, in which the speaker disarms the hostile audience by telling them that while they think he is going to say one thing, he is actually going to say another.

Mark Antony then delivers a speech that praises Caesar using ceremonial rhetoric (which he said he would not do), condemns Brutus using judicial rhetoric (which he said he would not do), and calls the crowd to avenge Caesar using deliberative rhetoric (which he said he would not do). He does all of these things, furthermore, without ever explicitly saying any of them. Such is the power—and danger—of rhetoric. What are these tools that Mark Antony makes such great use of?

Antony uses **irony**—saying one thing when you mean the opposite—with great effect. In written form, irony is very difficult to use well because the reader is more likely to take the word in its most literal sense. In spoken form, it is easier because the audience can hear the orator's tone. When Antony tells the audience "The noble Brutus/Hath told you Caesar was ambitious," and "For Brutus is an honorable man;/So are they all, all honorable men," he is using the terms "noble" and "honorable" ironically. Thus the audience's view of Brutus and the conspirators as noble and honorable men is subtly contradicted.

Paralipsis is a kind of irony that aids in undercutting the audience's beliefs. When Antony said he was not going to praise Caesar but then does, he is using paralipsis, which is when the orator says he is not going to discuss something but then manages to subtly communicate that thing anyway. Antony tells the crowd, "I speak not to disprove what Brutus spoke," and yet he effectively disproves Brutus's argument that Caesar was ambitious.

Erotema, also known as the rhetorical question, asks the audience a question with no intention of answering it aloud but with every intention of each audience member answering silently in his or her own mind. Antony asks, "I thrice presented him [Caesar] a kingly crown,/

Which he did thrice refuse: Was this ambition?" He gives enough information before asking the question to ensure that the audience will silently think of the correct answer after he asks the questions. He does it again a few lines later, "You all did love him once, not without cause:/What cause withholds you then, to mourn for him?" He gives the crowd just enough of a reminder of their prior love to ensure that they will answer his question the way he wants them to.

In Mark Antony's funeral oration, William Shakespeare gives us a rhetorical poem that moves us through the rhythms of Antony's thought. It connects us to ideas of truth, justice, and honor through the concrete realities that are Caesar's body, his coffin, and Antony's tears. Shakespeare also gives us poetic rhetoric that persuades us judicially, deliberatively, and ceremonially. It reveals both the genius of Shakespeare and the power and danger of rhetoric. Memorize at your own risk.

{poem}
The Agincourt Speech from *Henry V*

WESTMORELAND. O that we now had here
But one ten thousand of those men in England
That do no work to-day!

KING. What's he that wishes so?
My cousin Westmoreland? No, my fair cousin;
If we are mark'd to die, we are enow
To do our country loss; and if to live,
The fewer men, the greater share of honour.
God's will! I pray thee, wish not one man more.
By Jove, I am not covetous for gold,
Nor care I who doth feed upon my cost;
It yearns me not if men my garments wear;
Such outward things dwell not in my desires.
But if it be a sin to covet honour,
I am the most offending soul alive.
No, faith, my coz, wish not a man from England.
God's peace! I would not lose so great an honour
As one man more methinks would share from me
For the best hope I have. O, do not wish one more!
Rather proclaim it, Westmoreland, through my host,
That he which hath no stomach to this fight,
Let him depart; his passport shall be made,
And crowns for convoy put into his purse;
We would not die in that man's company

That fears his fellowship to die with us.
This day is call'd the feast of Crispian.
He that outlives this day, and comes safe home,
Will stand a tip-toe when this day is nam'd,
And rouse him at the name of Crispian.
He that shall live this day, and see old age,
Will yearly on the vigil feast his neighbours,
And say 'To-morrow is Saint Crispian.'
Then will he strip his sleeve and show his scars,
And say 'These wounds I had on Crispian's day.'
Old men forget; yet all shall be forgot,
But he'll remember, with advantages,
What feats he did that day. Then shall our names,
Familiar in his mouth as household words—
Harry the King, Bedford and Exeter,
Warwick and Talbot, Salisbury and Gloucester—
Be in their flowing cups freshly rememb'red.
This story shall the good man teach his son;
And Crispin Crispian shall ne'er go by,
From this day to the ending of the world,
But we in it shall be remembered—
We few, we happy few, we band of brothers;
For he to-day that sheds his blood with me
Shall be my brother; be he ne'er so vile,
This day shall gentle his condition;
And gentlemen in England now-a-bed
Shall think themselves accurs'd they were not here,
And hold their manhoods cheap whiles any speaks
That fought with us upon Saint Crispin's day.

{reflection}
Courage Is Contagious
by Anthony Esolen

It's a gray morning, and the French lords are on fire to fight, or so they say. They have spent the night like thoroughbred horses champing at the bit to attack. And they are right to be confident. The English, their enemies, are far from home. Their clothes are bedraggled. They have suffered hunger and cold. They have watched through the night, and we have seen their common soldiers before dawn, confident that they will see the sun rise but not that they will see it set. They are twelve thousand, against sixty thousand French.

At this point, in the English camp, the Earl of Westmoreland says something entirely reasonable. He wishes they had ten thousand more from England, "that do no work today." That would make the odds more even, for surely one Englishman is worth three Frenchmen! But King Henry overhears him and bursts forth with one of the most spirit-rousing fight-speeches ever uttered.

Numbers do not fight. Men fight, and strong hearts make strong arms. Henry knows it. He doesn't turn upon the earl but brings him in a friendly and jesting way into his own heart:

> *What's he that wishes so?*
> *My cousin Westmoreland? No, my fair cousin:*
> *If we are marked to die, we are enow*
> *To do our country loss; and if to live,*
> *The fewer men, the greater share of honor.*

If we die, we've got enough men here already to hurt our country, so in that case, we should wish for no more; but if we're going to live, well then, all the better that we are few! The honor we gain will be all the greater. And I, Henry, don't care much for fancy clothing—I'm a plain man that way; but if it's a sin to covet honor, "I am the most offending soul alive."

Courage is contagious—as is the joy of fighting. Throughout the previous scenes, we've seen Henry go about in disguise to hear what his men are thinking and to give them "a little touch of Harry in the night." Now he instills courage in all who hear him, and he does so with great bravado. Think of the surprise attack that Gideon mounted against the Midianites. God ordered Gideon to send home every man who had not the heart to fight, and even then the ranks were too large; and Gideon dismissed also every man who cupped his hands to drink from the stream, rather than leaning over eagerly and lapping it like a dog. Henry now makes a similar offer, and it is a personal thing as if every man were fighting within arm's length of the king himself:

That he which hath no stomach to this fight,
Let him depart; his passport shall be made,
And crowns for convoy put into his purse:
We would not die in that man's company
That fears his fellowship to die with us.

Suppose you are on one side of a crevasse in a glacier, a thousand feet straight down, and twelve feet separate you from the other side and home. If you look at your toes, if you gaze into the yawning abyss, you will never move an inch. You will search for another way. You will wander, persuading yourself that you are using your brains while the fog settles and the night comes on, and death is near, and all hope is lost. You must see past the deed, and that is what Henry has his audience do. It is Saint Crispin's Day? Well and good! Saint Crispin's Day will then be held sacred in future times. Henry does more than say so. He makes us feel it, living it in our imaginations and mingling the memory, not with grimness, but with whimsical humor and good cheer:

This day is call'd the feast of Crispian.
He that outlives this day, and comes safe home,
Will stand a tip-toe when this day is nam'd,
And rouse him at the name of Crispian.
He that shall live this day, and see old age,
Will yearly on the vigil feast his neighbours,
And say, 'To-morrow is Saint Crispian.'
Then will he strip his sleeve and show his scars,
And say, 'These wounds I had on Crispian's Day.'

Henry rings changes on the name of Crispin, as you might hear a platoon of great bells tolling out their names to proclaim a holy feast. Why, the veteran of Crispin's Day in time to come will keep a vigil—staying awake long into the night before, not in prayer and fasting but feasting with his friends. And can we not see the proud old man rolling up his sleeves and saying, "Boys, I was there, and these are the marks to prove it!"—his courage and faithfulness scored on his own flesh? Who would not want to be that man? And great things grow greater in old men's memories, says Henry with a smile:

> *Old men forget: yet all shall be forgot,*
> *But he'll remember, with advantages,*
> *What feats he did that day.*

But it is not a selfish thing. To fight with Henry, to take the odds of dying with Henry, is to be one with him and with his fellows. Their frank, ordinary, roast-beef English names, like the names of good old friends, enter a story that fathers pass down to their sons:

> *Then shall our names,*
> *Familiar in his mouth as household words—*
> *Harry the king, Bedford and Exeter,*
> *Warwick and Talbot, Salisbury and Gloucester—*
> *Be in their flowing cups freshly rememb'red.*
> *This story shall the good man teach his son . . .*

Even that is not the end. The king wants to assure himself and his men that their cause is just and blessed by God. And what we want then is to see the battle at Agincourt in the light of something that soars so far beyond the place and time, it touches upon eternity, and it brings together—as in one host of the blessed—men far apart in wealth and blood and rank:

> *And Crispin Crispian shall ne'er go by,*
> *From this day to the ending of the world,*
> *But we in it shall be remembered;*
> *We few, we happy few, we band of brothers;*
> *For he to-day that sheds his blood with me*
> *Shall be my brother; be he ne'er so vile,*
> *This day shall gentle his condition;*
> *And gentlemen in England now a-bed,*
> *Shall think themselves accurs'd they were not here,*
> *And hold their manhoods cheap whiles any speaks*
> *That fought with us upon Saint Crispin's day.*

By the end of this speech, every man is at least a knight, for we trust Henry will keep his promise; and the few are happy to be few, as brothers in a band, who all know one another and fight for one another with the far-seeing glint in the eye and a courage that does not count the cost. And Westmoreland himself, when the battle begins, and Henry asks him if he still wishes for more men, cries out,

> *God's will, my liege, would you and I alone,*
> *Without more help, could fight this royal battle!*

With hearts like those, what may not men dare to do?

{poem}

Portia's "The quality of mercy" speech in *The Merchant of Venice*

The quality of mercy is not strained.
It droppeth as the gentle rain from heaven
Upon the place beneath. It is twice blest:
It blesseth him that gives and him that takes.
'Tis mightiest in the mightiest; it becomes
The throned monarch better than his crown:
His scepter shows the force of temporal power,
The attribute to awe and majesty,
Wherein doth sit the dread and fear of kings;
But mercy is above this sceptered sway.
It is enthroned in the hearts of kings:
It is an attribute to God himself;
And earthly power doth then show likest God's
When mercy seasons justice. Therefore, Jew,
Though justice be thy plea, consider this:
That in the course of justice none of us
Should see salvation, we do pray for mercy.
And that same prayer doth teach us all to render
The deeds of mercy. I have spoke thus much
To mitigate the justice of thy plea,
Which if thou follow, this strict court of Venice
Must needs give sentence 'gainst the merchant there.

{reflection}
Portia's Unveiling
by Jessica Hooten Wilson

One of the great values of memorizing poetry is that another soul, with perhaps keener insight, may provide the words we need. Who has not felt overwhelmed by the emotion of a moment or oppressed by the moral confusion of a circumstance and needed truth to be dropped from on high into the heart and mind? Portia's speech from William Shakespeare's *The Merchant of Venice* does this when it clarifies the dissonance between mercy and justice. Her words are spoken in a Venetian court of law where she—in disguise as a man—acts as an advising attorney on behalf of the defendant and begs for a higher perspective on the facts. Within the context of the play, the speech occurs at the climax in act IV when the life of Antonio (an antiSemitic merchant) is jeopardized by his friend Bassanio's hyperbolic wager, "a pound of flesh," to which Bassanio consented with a wealthy

Jew, Shylock. The loan sounded like a joke, but Shylock intends to carry it out—to kill Antonio in reparation for the loan. Despite the eloquence of Portia's speech, Shylock persists. Only when Portia uses Shylock's literal hermeneutic against him must he relent: The bond is for flesh but not for a single ounce of blood. Portia saves her husband's friend from death by employing a more literal reading of the figurative bargain. While there are all sorts of ethical issues in this play worth discussing, the speech itself stands apart. Portia's call for mercy should be universal; to memorize this speech is to have, within one's soul, the wisdom to act as God might have us act.

Like all of Shakespeare's sonnets as well as lines of discourse between his higher-class characters, this speech is in iambic pentameter. In other words, five metrical feet that follow the rhythm te-TUM, te-TUM, te-TUM. Rather than add the final words of line fourteen, which include the particulars of Portia's denunciation of Shylock, the last line ends a foot early, concluding with her thesis. To memorize the poem, chant it to the rhythm of those feet. One could clap or tap or beat out the rhythm on her knee and begin to hear the verses metrically. One could almost sing this poem to the tune of "Amazing Grace" or "A Mighty Fortress Is Our God." Rhythmically, the poem echoes our most familiar way of speaking English. To hear someone deliver this speech, either watch the 2004 film, in which Lynn Collins plays Portia (also with Al Pacino, Joseph Fiennes, and Jeremy Irons), or download an audiobook version.

If you rewrite Portia's speech into sentences without their poetic line breaks, you may be able to grasp the argument that she makes. Knowing the substance of her argument will help you memorize her words. In the first sentence, which comprises two clauses connected with a semicolon, Portia argues that one cannot overextend mercy or "strain" its quality because it is not of earthly origin. While humans assume limits on mercy (that it would be "strained" if offered broadly), Portia directs her listeners to a higher source, "heaven," from which mercy drops as gentle rain and twice blesses—to the giver and receiver. In this second sentence, which expands upon the image of rain in line two, Portia fortifies the quality of mercy. While it may drop as "gentle" rain, we should not misconstrue it as weak. Rather, " '[t]is mightiest in the mightiest." Portia continues this second sentence for the rest of the poem, elaborating on the heavenly might that provides mercy with its strength.

Although, within the context of the play, the verses construct an argument, they also retain the elements of a poem, employing internal rhyme that ties the lines together and may provide help in remembering how one line follows another. While each line does not end on a rhyme, the final word of line one—"strained"—rhymes with the next line's "rain" then the emphatic "a" sound continues in "place" and "takes" in the next two lines. A new rhyme begins in line three with the high "I" in "twice" repeated in line five: "mightiest in the mightiest." Line six switches to the low "o" sound "throned" that then rhymes with "shows" of line seven. This rhyme is repeated in lines eleven and thirteen with "enthroned" and "show."

Portia repeats not only sounds in her speeches but words as well—to contrast our earthly understanding with the divine meaning of these ideas. She repeats words such as "attribute" and "power" to contrast that of the earthly monarch with the King of kings. Lines six, seven, eight, and nine employ the words "throne," "scepter," "temporal power," and "attribute," which are the "dread and fear of kings," referring to earthly rulers. These words or phrases are repeated in lines ten, eleven, twelve, and thirteen with "sceptered," "enthroned," "hearts of kings," "attribute," and "earthly power," but their meaning is overturned in these instances in light of divine interpretation. Portia emphasizes her move from earth to heaven by repeating the syntactical form "It is" in lines eleven and twelve: "It is enthroned ..." and "It is an attribute ..." The word "mercy" from line one is repeated finally in line fourteen, but what began as an object of a preposition in a passive construction concludes as the active subject of the final clause, seasoning (or tempering) "justice."

One should remember that Portia, although a noble woman, delivers this poem under the guise of a man, speaking only to men. Shakespeare would have written this play in deference to Queen Elizabeth I, who held what had been for centuries a male-only position. Her half-sister Mary had only ruled for five years before her, as the first woman to lead the nation in its history (the nine-day rule of Lady Jane Grey, notwithstanding). Several hundred years later, Virginia Woolf observed (in *A Room of One's Own*) the conflict between women within Shakespeare's plays and their historical position:

> *"[I]f woman had no existence save in the fiction written by men, one would imagine her a person of the utmost importance ... But this is woman in fiction. In fact, as Professor Trevelyan [who wrote The History of England] points out, she was locked up, beaten and flung about the room."*

Whereas Portia has the opportunity to articulate these thoughts within the fictitious universe of Shakespeare's Venice, in reality, only the Queen would have been able to convey such sentiment, and her privilege to do so was new.

Why is this context important for memorizing this speech? Because women in the twenty-first century in many Western countries may now address—to audiences of women and men alike—these beautiful and wise words without the necessity of a mask and without fear of being beaten. To memorize Portia's speech is to give voice to women who have been and are silenced by the brokenness of our culture. It is to temper earthly notions of justice with divine mercy. The speech reminds us to strive to act "likest God" in our interactions with one another, most especially for those of us who have been placed in positions of power within our culture. By memorizing and reciting these words, one embodies the lessons of mercy, blessing not only she who speaks but also the one who listens.

{poem}
Sonnet 29

When, in disgrace with fortune and men's eyes,
I all alone beweep my outcast state,
And trouble deaf heaven with my bootless cries,
And look upon myself and curse my fate,
Wishing me like to one more rich in hope,
Featured like him, like him with friends possessed,
Desiring this man's art and that man's scope,
With what I most enjoy contented least;
Yet in these thoughts myself almost despising,
Haply I think on thee, and then my state,
(Like to the lark at break of day arising
From sullen earth) sings hymns at heaven's gate;
    For thy sweet love remembered such wealth brings
    That then I scorn to change my state with kings.

{reflection}
Love Rescues the Soul
by Ian Andrews

Sonnet 29 is far from Shakespeare's deepest love poem. It lacks some of the sparkling word play of Sonnet 116 and some of the profundity of Sonnet 104. It does, however, present us with a fine example of his favorite form and one of his most memorable closing lines, making it an excellent poem to add to your repertoire.

Sonnet 29 participates in a larger cycle of poems intended to be read sequentially, and, for that reason, it may be helpful to read some of the poems that precede it for context. Nearly all of Shakespeare's one hundred fifty-four sonnets are meditations on the effect of romantic love—no matter how shallow and foolish—and on the emotions of the poet. Sonnet 29, however, joins a comparatively fewer number of sonnets that explore a higher topic—true love's power to affect the poet's outlook on the world and even the state of his eternal soul.

As in all sonnets, Shakespeare presents the reader with a problem, explained in this case over the first four lines: He has fallen victim to ill fortune, and neither heaven nor his fellow man are moved by his suffering. He "beweep[s his] outcast state" all alone, with "bootless [useless] cries" that no one hears. While we aren't told precisely what manner of ill-fortune afflicts him, we are given some clue as to its impact on his heart, beginning in line five. He is not only disappointed by his bad luck, but also feels he alone is the target of fate's ill will. As he casts his eyes about, he sees other men enjoying the fruit of their labors and sinks into envy, comparing himself in every facet of his life to one "more rich in hope." This jealousy ultimately saps his contentment in everything he does, including that which he most enjoys: his art. During the turn of the poem, in line nine, the poet punctuates this bleak diagnosis of his state with a frank aside: "in these thoughts myself almost despising." Whereas in the first several lines, he fingers fortune as the villain, he here admits that the true target of his dissatisfaction is his own malaise. He cannot love the hopeless man he sees in the mirror.

At last, however, a chance thought of the poet's lover dawns, piercing his dark night of the soul. No longer does he languish in self-pity; but instead, gloriously aware of the gift of love he has been given, he sings praises at the gate of the very heaven that was a few lines earlier "deaf" to his complaints. Not only is his art—his own personal lark's song—given back to him in all its power, but his perspective on the world shifts entirely from self-centered myopia to an all-encompassing gratitude.

When he searches in his own heart for meaning and validation, he returns empty and jaded. But when he looks at his life through the lens of relationship, he would rather be himself, poor as he is, than any literal or metaphorical "king." Love rescues the poet's soul from base concerns about money, fame, and personal gratification, affirming the primacy of human connection and intimacy over the trappings of worldly security.

As you go about memorizing this poem, a formal understanding of its structure will be immensely helpful, particularly as Shakespeare tweaks his sonnet form in creative ways to emphasize the idea at the heart of the poem. Sonnet 29, like all sonnets, consists of a single, fourteen-line stanza— groups of four lines and a final couplet. A reader could be forgiven for further expecting the traditional rhyme scheme ABABCDCCDEFEFGG. Instead, Shakespeare varies that structure, repeating the B rhyme ("state") in the third group, and the E rhyme ("despising") in the final couplet for a new rhyme scheme— ABABCDCDEBEBEE.

This rhyme scheme draws the reader's attention to the pivotal shift in the poet's perception of the world—while the first "state" rhymes with a cursed "fate" and clearly reflects the poet's dissatisfaction with his physical circumstances, the second is likened to a lark's song sung to heaven itself. This transition from a worldly definition of wealth to a spiritual one anchors the tone of the poem. Thus the recitation should reflect the poet's dolorous tone in the first eight lines, before— beginning with the word "yet" in line nine—lifting triumphantly.

In addition, the four instances of the B end-rhyme should function as aural signposts for memorization—"state," "fate," "state," "gate." These two sections bracket the four middle lines and build to the crescendo of the final couplet.

Percy Bysshe Shelley
1792–1822

Best known for: "Ozymandias,"
"Ode to the West Wind," "To a Skylark"

A major English Romantic poet, Shelley was born in 1792 in West Sussex, England to wealthy and aristocratic parents. Although his early childhood was idyllic, he fared badly at Eton College where he was tormented by older boys and made no friends. After matriculation, he enrolled at University College, Oxford, where he attended only one lecture during his entire college career but read sixteen hours a day. His Oxford writings establish him as a talented but outspoken young poet with radical political and social ideas. After being expelled in his second year at Oxford for publishing pamphlets espousing atheism and radicalism, Shelley embarked on a literary career. Shelley married twice—both elopements—first at age nineteen to sixteen-year-old Harriet Westbrook, who bore him two children before drowning herself while in late pregnancy in 1816. After Harriet's death, he immediately married Mary Godwin, the daughter of philosopher William Godwin and activist Mary Wollstonecraft. This famous literary marriage was characterized by the tumultuous intensity, alternating between heights of connected intimacy and creative genius on the one hand with depths of hysterical conflict and cruel betrayals on the other. Shelley was a masterful Romantic poet who crafted his intense melancholy and original thought into a prolific body of work. Shelley drowned in a boating accident right before his thirtieth birthday.

{poem}
Ozymandias

I met a traveller from an antique land,
Who said—"Two vast and trunkless legs of stone
Stand in the desert. . . . Near them, on the sand,
Half sunk a shattered visage lies, whose frown,
And wrinkled lip, and sneer of cold command,
Tell that its sculptor well those passions read
Which yet survive, stamped on these lifeless things,
The hand that mocked them, and the heart that fed;
And on the pedestal, these words appear:
My name is Ozymandias, King of Kings;
Look on my Works, ye Mighty, and despair!
Nothing beside remains. Round the decay
Of that colossal Wreck, boundless and bare
The lone and level sands stretch far away."

{reflection}

A Royal Mockery
by Anthony Esolen

People sometimes suppose that writing can't be poetry unless the language is highly wrought with weird curlicues and grotesque images and at best a passing familiarity with ordinary grammar. That, of course, is nonsense. And sometimes, as we see in Percy Bysshe Shelley's sonnet, "Ozymandias," the poetry consists in not being "poetical" but restrained, tacit—suggesting much by saying little but making sure that every least feature of that little counts. The very stones cry out, and so do the empty spaces between the stones.

In the first line, Shelley leads us to believe that we will hear about something quaint or romantic from that "antique" land—not merely ancient but antique, old in a magical way. No such thing. The two dead words beginning the second line, "Who said," with the abrupt dash that sets them off, leave us instead in a world where tourists wander—weary tourists. Indeed, what follows sounds as if it could come either from a world-weary fellow or from an oracle who has gained his wisdom at much cost—or from both as they are the same man.

What does the traveler tell of? Old and venerable temples or statues of goddesses fresh as the west wind and lovely as trees in bloom? Not hardly. "Two vast and trunkless legs of stone/Stand in the desert," he says. We are dealing here with a colossus, an enormous statue of the human form such as once guarded the harbor of Rhodes. The bronze statue at Rhodes, as tall as the Statue of Liberty, was of the god Apollo, protector of the island, and was built by a free people to commemorate their victory over the more powerful Cypriots. That colossus is not like this colossus. Here we have a ruler who erected a colossus of himself to proclaim his tyranny over his own people and to threaten anyone or anything that would oppose him. The Rhodians celebrated liberty. The nameless slaves who were dragooned into erecting this statue had nothing to celebrate. Cringing is not celebration.

This statue, now, is an absurdity. It would be less absurd if the legs were lying on the sand. They stand, trunkless, a mockery of the human form. The traveler doesn't tell us where the trunk lies. Probably in the desert sand in this nowhere, this dry nothingness, covered up forever. We do see the thing's face—or part of it. It is a "shattered visage," half sunk into the sand. The face testifies to the soul within. What is the soul of the despot?

Here we come to the drama of the poem, understated and more powerful for being so. Imagine a sculptor at work, one who knows his business. He reads this despot and reads him well. He sees the passions at work, and he chisels them into the stone—in the "frown,/ And wrinkled lip, and sneer of cold command." Would that offend the despot? Not likely. His heart may feed those passions, but his own hand mocks them. He does not pretend to be other than he is: a man who rules and who sneers as he does so.

Finally the statue speaks in the inscription of the pedestal, which puts in words what appears without words on the shattered face:

> *My name is Ozymandias, King of Kings;*
> *Look on my Works, ye Mighty, and despair!*

These two lines are master strokes of dramatic irony, which involves a clash of levels of knowledge or ignorance among actors in a scene or between an actor and the audience that watches. Let's try to enumerate the ironies here. Ozymandias said those words when he commanded the sculptor to engrave them upon the pedestal—when he thought that the memorial to his power would endure forever. But it did not endure, and now it is the pedestal alone, that base for legs broken at the thighs, that speaks them to an empty wilderness. Ozymandias should have known that it must eventually be so, but he was struck blind by his arrogance.

Our traveler names the despot. It is Ozymandias, the Greek rendering for a name given to Rameses II, one of the mightiest and most warlike pharaohs of Egypt. All at once we are in history, and indeed Shelley has taken his inscription from the ancient traveler Diodorus Siculus, who saw it on a colossal statue of Rameses. Why did Shelley's traveler not tell us so at first? Why he did not want us to identify the statue right away? Because we are to think about what the statue means before we can locate it in a time or place. And the name Ozymandias would, unlike Rameses, be unfamiliar even to most of Shelley's learned readers. The name thus cuts its own feet off from underneath itself. If he is the King of Kings, why have we never heard of him?

But if we do understand that he is Rameses II, the irony grows bitterer still. For he was commonly held to be the pharaoh from whom God delivered the children of Israel when his chariots and charioteers followed the slaves into the Red Sea, and the waters rushed back upon them and drowned them all. Thus the most memorable thing about Rameses is that defeat—at the hand of a God who raises the lowly and puts down their oppressors. Rameses calls himself "King of Kings," but Shelley's readers would have thought instead of the triumphant Christ putting down the wicked rulers of the world: "And he hath on his vesture and on his thigh a name written, King of Kings, and Lord of Lords" (Rev. 19:16 [KJV]). Shelley was no believing Christian, but his heart was with Christ the liberator and not with the world's imperial powers.

"Look on my Works, ye Mighty, and despair!" Brilliant irony, that. It is not only that the statue has nothing to brag of now; it is that it delivers a prophecy and not the one that Rameses intended. You should despair, ye Mighty—not that Ozymandias is greater than you but that you are and will ever be no more than what Ozymandias now is: a mockery, a trunkless statue in a desert. "Nothing beside remains," says the traveler, not even the ruins of a city wall. "[B]oundless and bare,/The lone and level sands stretch far away."

Does the poet draw the lesson out? No. The wreck is the lesson.

A. E. Stallings
1968–

Best known for: Archaic Smile, Like,
Works and Days *(translation)*

American poet and translator Alicia Elsbeth Stallings studied classics at the University of Georgia and Latin Literature at the University of Oxford. Her first collection of poetry, *Archaic Smile*, was published in 1999 to widespread critical acclaim. Since then, she has published three more collections: *Hapax* (2006), *Olives* (2012), and *Like* (2018). Her work is associated with New Formalism, a literary movement dedicated to the resurgence of traditional forms in contemporary poetics. Unlike many New Formalists, however, who contemplate modern life within the framework of established forms, Stallings' formalism is unique. While maintaining strict attention to the appropriate boundaries of form, Stallings at the same time demonstrates the playfulness of true mastery, fluidly adapting elements of structure and language to craft poetry that relies more on internal harmony than rigid tradition. "For all of Stallings' formal virtuosity, few of her poems are strictly metrically regular," wrote reviewer A. M. Juster. "Indeed, one of the pleasant surprises of *Archaic Smile* is the number of superb poems in the gray zone between free and blank verse." Her education as a classicist adds nuanced depths of metaphor and allusion to her poetry. In addition to her career as a poet, Stallings is also a celebrated translator. She published a 2007 verse translation of Lucretius' *De Rerum Natura (On the Nature of Things)* and a 2018 verse translation of Hesiod's *Works and Days*. More recent work includes various articles exploring the refugee crisis in Greece where Stallings lives and works with her husband and two children.

{poem}

Listening to *Peter and the Wolf* with Jason, Aged Three

Eyes wide open, grinning ear to ear,
Balanced between the thrill of fear and fear,
He clutches at my skirt to keep me near

And will not let me leave him by himself
In the living room where *Peter and the Wolf*
Emerges from the speakers on the shelf.

He likes Peter's jaunty swing of strings,
The reedy waddle of the duck, the wings
That flute up in the tree, but still he clings,

(Even though for now it's just the cat
Picking its sneaky way through sharp and flat);
He isn't frightened of a clarinet,

And laughs at Grandfather's bluster and bassoon,
But keeps his ear out for another tune
At the shadowy edge of the wood, and coming soon.

Where is the wolf? he asks me every chance
He gets, and I explain each circumstance;
Though it's not as if he's heard it only once—

You'd think he'd know by now. *Deep in the wood,*
Or under the tree, or sent away for good
To the zoo, I say, and think he's understood,

And weary of the question and the classic,
I ask *him* where the wolf is. With grave logic,
He answers me, "The wolf is in the music."

And so it is. Just then, out of the gloom
The cymbal menaces, the French horns loom.
And the music is loose. The music's in the room.

{reflection}

The Hope of Unknowing
by Jeffrey Bilbro

A. E. Stallings grew up in Georgia and moved to Greece after studying the classics in college. She has translated various classics—most recently Hesiod's *Works and Days*—while writing her own poetry. One strand that runs through her work is the faith that old myths, stories, and forms continue to speak to contemporary culture. Like the musical composition to which it responds, "Listening to *Peter and the Wolf* with Jason, Aged Three" is a whimsical and delightful celebration of art's almost magical power: The stories we tell in both music and poetry don't stay demurely on the page—when performed, they leap forth and take on a life of their own. Memorizing and reciting Stallings' poem provides a rich opportunity to experience this mystery for yourself.

To understand this poem, it helps to know a bit about the musical piece referred to in the title: Sergei Prokofiev's beloved classic *Peter and the Wolf* (1936). Prokofiev called it a "symphonic fairy tale for children," and it intersperses a spoken narrative with musical interludes. If you've never heard it, it's certainly worth looking up a performance. Over the course of about thirty minutes, Prokofiev introduces his audience to a few of the many instrumental voices that make up an orchestra: The flute voices the bird; the oboe, the duck; the clarinet, the cat; the bassoon, the grandfather; the strings, Peter; the French horns, the wolf; and the drums, the shooting of the hunter's rifles.

While Prokofiev's piece is now used to introduce children to the various instruments that make up an orchestra, its original audience likely heard it as a Soviet fable lauding the initiative and courage of youthful Pioneers and poking fun at the stodgy, anti-revolutionary older generation. Prokofiev initially titled the piece, *How Pioneer Pe ter Caught the Wolf.* The Pioneers were a Soviet version of the Boy Scouts and Girl Scouts, and Peter comes off as the canny and resourceful hero of the story.

The narrative begins as Peter opens the yard gate and goes out for a walk in the large meadow. The duck takes advantage of the open gate and heads for the pond. On the way, the duck gets into an argument with a bird about whether real avians can swim or fly (apparently the domesticated duck had her wings clipped and so cannot fly). While the two fowl are arguing, Peter spots the cat stalking them and calls out a warning; the bird then flies into a tree, and the duck swims to the middle of the pond. At this juncture, Peter's grandfather finds Peter and angrily commands him to return to the yard and shut the gate. After they leave the meadow, the wolf makes his entrance. His presence so terrifies the duck that she leaps out of the pond and is gulped down by the hungry wolf. In spite of the duck's demise and his grandfather's warnings, Peter is not afraid. He gets a rope, climbs the wall, and scampers along an overhanging branch into the same tree. From here, he lowers a lasso and, while the bird flies around the wolf's head to distract him, catches the wolf's tail. The hunters enter at this point, and Peter enlists them to help him secure the wolf. The song ends with Peter leading a triumphant procession, taking the wolf to the zoo.

In Prokofiev's story, the duck and the grandfather come off as the staid and cowardly fools while Peter and the bird are the daring heroes: their spirit of adventure and boldness leads to their success over the wolf. In Stallings' poem, however, the wolf cannot be tamed. Its presence in the room with her and her son marks the surprise turn near the end of the poem and lends the concluding lines their power.

Stallings is a master of the poetic craft, so not only is the poem written in formal verse—iambic pentameter set in rhyming tercets— but it also mimics the timbre of the various musical instruments. When reciting the poem, you can make each animal's description sound like their particular instrumental motifs: the "reedy waddle of the duck" is voiced in the middle of the mouth and at a lower register than the "flute up in the tree," all of which—with the sole exception of the last vowel sound—is said, flute-like, at the front of the mouth with the lips and teeth. The assonance in "Peter's jaunty swing of strings" invites a dance-like confidence, and the alliterative plosives of "Grandfather's bluster and bassoon" convey his bold and angry demeanor.

Given its vivid and varied voices, Stallings' poem follows Prokofiev's composition in being dramatic: it stages different voices in a brief scene. The two main characters are the mother and her three-year-old son, but their conversation is shaped in response to the musical cast. At the outset, the poet portrays herself as the exasperated mother, frustrated by the fact that her son's fears make him cling to her skirts. Further, the mother is "weary" of both her son's insistent queries and the song—she and her son have heard it many times before—and so, as parents are wont to do, she finally responds to her son's pestering questions by turning them back on him: Where do you think the wolf is? And the three-year-old's answer is profound in the literalistic way common to children: "'The wolf is in the music.'"

The poem turns on this simple declaration. From the beginning, the son is thrilled by his fear: he is "grinning" while "[b]alanced between the thrill of fear and fear." But it is only when his reply shifts the mother's perspective that she, too, can experience the delightful frisson of fear, hearing the wolf stalk into the room on the notes of the French horns. If Prokofiev's Peter tames the wolf, then Jason, aged three, sets him loose.

Thus it is the poet herself who experiences the enchanting, transformative power of language; her son's statement utterly alters her understanding of the music. Instead of being bored by the music, she now hears the wolf's palpable presence. And this is the power of poetry. By narrating and giving meaning to our experiences, it can help us better understand their true complexity and mystery. Though we may be tempted to use language to tame life, this poem invites us to see language as a way of discovering life's true wildness. The mother is in danger of discounting this musical experience with her son. Like most mothers, she likely has many other matters she needs to deal with. But Jason's simple phrase, like good poetry and good music, wakes her up to the marvels of life. Reciting this poem can remind others—and ourselves!—that attending to the voices of those around us, even the voice of an annoyingly insistent three-year-old, can transform our perspective.

Wallace Stevens
1879–1955

Best known for: "The Idea of Order at Key West,"
"Disillusionment of Ten O'Clock," "The Auroras of Autumn"

In 1923 poet and critic Mark Van Doren wrote that Wallace Stevens' debut collection, *Harmonium*, "is tentative, perverse, and superfine; and it will never be popular." It sold just one hundred copies, and so it seemed that Van Doren was right. Only a few years later, however, Stevens emerged as one of the most compelling poetic voices of the century. Stevens was a modernist poet who, having been educated at Harvard and New York Law School, worked as an executive at a Connecticut insurance company. Poetry was his leisure activity, and he was one of the rare great poets whose work emerged past middle age. *Harmonium* was published when he was in his forties, and his most well-regarded work was published when he was in his fifties or older. His work is complex and highly philosophical and thus can be difficult to interpret, but it's also some of the most precise and beautiful verse written in the last one hundred years. So although Van Doren may have been right to some degree—Stevens may never be truly popular among the general public—it's also worth noting that Harold Bloom called him "the best and most representative American poet of our time."

{poem}
The House Was Quiet and the World Was Calm

The house was quiet and the world was calm.
The reader became the book; and summer night

Was like the conscious being of the book.
The house was quiet and the world was calm.

The words were spoken as if there was no book,
Except that the reader leaned above the page,

Wanted to lean, wanted much most to be
The scholar to whom his book is true, to whom

The summer night is like a perfection of thought.
The house was quiet because it had to be.

The quiet was part of the meaning, part of the mind:
The access of perfection to the page.

And the world was calm. The truth in a calm world,
In which there is no other meaning, itself

Is calm, itself is summer and night, itself
Is the reader leaning late and reading there.

{reflection}

When the Reptitions Lead the Way

by David Kern

As I write, I am sitting at a large wooden table, books and notebooks and pens and coffee and water and a bowl of cherries spread around me. It's quiet—unusually quiet for someone with four young children. My watch is ticking, an appliance hums tentatively across the room, and, in the distance, I can hear a train's faint rumbling. I'm writing longhand, on sketch paper as is my custom, and my computer is turned off. It's an Airbnb, rented for a few days to give me a chance at getting some real work done. No distractions, just books and words (and coffee, of course). I've spent my day with my nose buried in poetry and fiction, thinking deeply, looking for connections, asking questions, and attempting to put into words and onto paper what meager insights I am given. I've paced; I've lain on the sofa; I've sat on the table top with my feet on the chair; I've done pushups and made more coffee; and mostly I've struggled with the painful process of writing, that is—more generally speaking—the life of the mind.

These are the conditions, which Wallace Stevens seems to be suggesting are necessary for thought that leads to real discovery, that he describes in "The House Was Quiet and the World Was Calm." Of course, modern man that I am, I find myself wanting to check on the hockey game, to put on some jazz, and to check my email. It's difficult to pay close attention to complicated things for a long time—to push the distractions and concerns of the world out and be single-minded. That is true even when the time to do so with purpose has been set aside. But in Stevens' estimation, it is worth the effort.

"The House Was Quiet and the World Was Calm" is a rich poem that feels complicated primarily because it buries its core themes in repetition—by using multiple names for the same ideas. In this, it demands the sort of close attention that the poem advocates. It also employs both simile and metaphor in a playful and expert fashion.

With its opening line, the poem describes the necessary conditions for that attention to take place: "The house was quiet and the world was calm." The scene is contemplative, restful, and peaceful—both within the house itself and in the world outside of it. And with that setting in place, transformation can occur: "The reader became the book." Surely one of the most memorable examples of metaphor in American poetry, the line is striking for its simplicity and provocative for how unusual it is. But most interesting is the way the use of metaphor itself (as opposed to the similes used elsewhere in the poem) suggests meaning. "The reader became the book," we're told. That is, the reader becomes one with the book and the book one with the reader. The reader doesn't become like the book; the reader and the book merge. In the quiet of the house, the reader is transformed. But then it is as if the book itself comes alive, is transformed itself, for the poet tells us that the "summer night/Was like the conscious being of the book." So the reader has become the book, and the book comes alive in the summer night, and the reader thus is both book and summer night. Stevens then completes the thought by repeating the opening line. The three have merged into one, and it is the quiet that leads the way.

Throughout the rest of the poem, Stevens uses these parameters to contemplate the ephemeral nature of consciousness and the relationship between revelation and physical human experience. He speaks of words spoken (presumably aloud), of the reader leaning over the book, and of the presence of the page on which the words are written. For it is the page—the actual physical artifact—that grounds the words and the ideas they express in human experience and that keeps the book itself moored to present reality and that allows the words and the reader to merge.

When the poem talks of a reader who "[w]anted to lean, wanted much most to be/The scholar to whom his book is true," it speaks of the urgency of the search for truth. The reader leans over the page, hunting for clues and for knowledge. Perhaps, like me, you're the kind of reader who paces, who lies down, then who stands up. For all of us, in some way, the search Stevens contemplates is expressed through manifestly physical means, embodied in the interaction of our bodies with the artifacts we are contemplating. In fact, the final four lines of the poem tell us that "truth in a calm world ... itself is summer and night ... itself/Is the reader leaning late and reading there." The truth is the book come alive—the consciousness of the book represented by summer and night—as we grapple with it and hunt and study and seek a "perfection of thought" that is accessible only through the quest; without the quiet, there is no access to the consciousness of the book, no thing to awaken, and no access to the ephemeral core of the artifact we lean over or walk with or bring to the sofa.

The cyclical nature of this poem—the mathematical, musical form it employs—offers memorizers a deeply satisfying experience. The repetitions mark the movement, like a chorus come round again or a common denominator, but they're not there just to keep you awake as you contemplate. They're there to provide something to grasp on to. As Susan Smith Nash wrote about this poem, these repetitions "heighten the transformation process." The repetitions lead the way.

In his new book, *The Soul Is a Stranger In This World: Essays on Poets and Poetry*, Micah Mattix writes that "what mattered most to Stevens was poetry's power to capture the 'passions of rain' and subdue the 'unsubdued/elations when the forest blooms.' He hoped to give language a richness and density and to give the quotidian a strangely evocative newness—a philosophical weight." That is exactly what Stevens accomplishes in "The House Was Quiet and the World Was Calm." But it's also what each of us seek to do when we spread our books and our notebooks and our pens and our coffee on the table, when we turn off the game and close the email, when we let the quiet come alive as we lean over some words worth wrestling with, when we pace and lie down and sit on the table-top with our feet on the chair, and when we brew that next cup of coffee. Even, I think, when we commit those words to memory.

Poets Who Had "Regular" Jobs

Famously, Wallace Stevens worked for many years as an executive at an insurance company, a job he kept even as he saw success with his writing. But Stevens is far from the only poet to keep a "regular"* day job (whatever that means) while hammering away at lines. Here are a few more, with a poem worth memorizing:

William Carlos Williams worked as a family physican for more than forty years in his native Rutherford, New Jersey. A leading figure in the Imagist movement, his work is known as formally experimental even as it was inspired by rather conventional, quotidian matters. Memorize: "The Red Wheelbarrow."

Like Stevens, American poet **Ted Kooser** was a vice president for an insurance company where he worked while steadily building up an admirable canon of poems, ultimately leading to his selection as Poet Laureate Consultant in Poetry to the Library of Congress from 2004 to 2006. Memorize: "Abandoned Farmhouse."

Walt Whitman, one of the most influential of all American poets, worked as government clerk (thanks to a letter of recommendation from Ralph Waldo Emerson). So the poet whom Ezra Pound once declared as "America's poet" started as a low-level bureaucrat. Anything is possible. Memorize: "A Noiseless Patient Spider."

*Also consider every great poet whose "regular" job was: mother, farmer, soldier, teacher,

W. B. Yeats
1865–1939

Best known for: "The Lake Isle of Innisfree," "Second Coming,"
"Sailing to Byzantium," "The Wild Swans at Coole"

Probably the greatest of all Irish poets, William Butler Yeats was the 1923 recipient of the Nobel Prize in Literature and was, for many poets of the twentieth century, a leading inspiration. In fact, in 1948, W. H. Auden wrote an essay for *The Kenyon Review* called "Yeats As an Example" in which he argued that Yeats was the author of "some of the most beautiful poetry" ever written in the English language. In the images he employed, the subjects he wrote about, and the ideas he proposed, Yeats' work was obsessed with Ireland and with Irish ways of living in an ever-changing world—but his greatest poems are as meaningful today as they were in his own time because, in examining the Irish experience, they diagnosed the complex spiritual state of the modern age. His career was long and his interests varied, and thus his work evolved both formally and conceptually such that his canon grew into one of the most interesting and essential collections of poetry ever written.

{poem}
Sailing to Byzantium

I

That is no country for old men. The young
In one another's arms, birds in the trees,
—Those dying generations—at their song,
The salmon-falls, the mackerel-crowded seas,
Fish, flesh, or fowl, commend all summer long
Whatever is begotten, born, and dies.
Caught in that sensual music all neglect
Monuments of unageing intellect.

II

An aged man is but a paltry thing,
A tattered coat upon a stick, unless
Soul clap its hands and sing, and louder sing
For every tatter in its mortal dress,
Nor is there singing school but studying
Monuments of its own magnificence;
And therefore I have sailed the seas and come
To the holy city of Byzantium.

III

O sages standing in God's holy fire
As in the gold mosaic of a wall,
Come from the holy fire, perne in a gyre,
And be the singing masters of my soul.
Consume my heart away; sick with desire
And fastened to a dying animal
It knows not what it is; and gather me
Into the artifice of eternity.

IV

Once out of nature I shall never take
My bodily form from any natural thing,
But such a form as Grecian goldsmiths make
Of hammered gold and gold enamelling
To keep a drowsy Emperor awake;
Or set upon a golden bough to sing
To lords and ladies of Byzantium
Of what is past, or passing, or to come.

{reflection}

A Curious Alchemy
by Heidi White

William Butler Yeats published "Sailing to Byzantium" in his 1928 collection, *The Tower*, while in his early sixties. In this season of his later work, the Irish poet often explored his ambivalence about aging, both as an individual and as a citizen of a world in flux. Known for his Irish nationalism, Yeats wrote mournful poetry not only to express his own personal longings and losses but also on behalf of his beloved and beleaguered homeland, plagued by violence and division. His later work became less nationalistic but not less political. Rather, he expanded his political vision to explore his longing for an enduring individual and national order. To symbolize this longing, Yeats chose the ancient city of Byzantium, a city that had long captivated his prodigious imagination.

Like all great poetry, Yeats' work functions on multiple levels of meaning: Many of his poems at this late stage contemplate how the aging of the body and the undulations of history are mirrors of one another. He forged mystical links between his personal angst about growing old and his obsession with ancient spiritual traditions, particularly those of the Byzantine East. To Yeats, Byzantium was more than a lost city of the past; it was a symbol of glory and desire, gone forever in the fading of the years. The elusive ideal of Byzantium carried the weight of Yeats' ever-intensifying longing to remember—and somehow to recover—a bygone Golden Age.

Yeats wrote with a curious alchemy of formal restraint and intricate meaning, a dynamic that pervades "Sailing to Byzantium." Formally, the poem is a compact four-stanza poem written in ***ottava rima***: stanzas of eight, ten-syllable lines. The meter comprises nearly flawless iambic pentameter with a regular rhyme scheme of ABABACDD. The elegance of its compact form juxtaposes the complexity of its dense content, creating a poem that is easy to memorize yet fathomless to contemplate.

The poem tells the story of the narrator's metaphorical odyssey from the callow, modern landscape to the ancient art and wisdom of Byzantium. The speaker mourns, in the famous opening line, that the modern world is "no country for old men." Yeats was known for his vivid and complex symbolism, which we see in the stanza's two fecund images of modern life: "salmon-falls" and "mackerel-crowded seas." Like salmon, the young are ever multiplying and ever thrashing haphazardly up a churning and chaotic current. The speaker no longer feels at home in such a world. "And therefore I have sailed the seas and come/To the holy city of Byzantium." The aging man abandons the visceral world in pursuit of his ideal.

In Byzantium, he encounters a series of images suffused with symbolic meaning: a gold mosaic of wise men standing in a sacred fire (a symbol of purified wisdom), thread rotating upon a spinning wheel ("perne in a gyre," a symbol of the cyclical patterns of history), and a mechanical golden bird on a golden bough (a symbol of the declarative function of art). Byzantium, we discover, is a world of art. The five-fold repetition of the word "gold" communicates the inherent glory and value of the city's creative culture, forcing upon us that Yeats' idealized city is artistic rather than organic. In fact, so vehement is the old man's rejection of his aging body that he declares, "Once out of nature I shall never take/My bodily form from any natural thing," but instead he will become a golden bird upon a golden bough, forever singing songs "[o]f what is past, or passing, or to come." The narrator, enamored with artistic endeavor, will himself become a work of art declaring the city's undying glory beyond the grave.

Yeats' symbolism is not merely visual but aural. The motif of singing permeates the poem. In the first stanza, the voices of living birds represent the "dying generations" while in the second stanza the old man disdains his own soul, which sings "[f]or every tatter in its mortal dress." The speaker longs for "singing-masters of my soul" who will teach him to perform eternal harmonies. In Byzantium, he will find the "singing school" he longs for so that, upon his death, he can transform from old man to golden bird. The dying-while-living bird of the first stanza gives way to the artificial—but eternal—bird of the final one. This reiterates the poem's elevation of art above life, offering art as a potential solution to the problem of encroaching individual and cultural death. The endless cycles of emergence and decay cannot be avoided, but perhaps they can be preserved in arrested motion through the "artifice of eternity." Since the poem itself is a sublime work of art composed in melodious syllables of lilting musicality, it takes on a haunted unity of grief and hope—as if Yeats is offering it as the song for the mechanical bird to sing for all eternity while perching on the golden bough.

Yeats is known as the last great Romantic poet, so it perhaps seems strange that the poem glorifies the "artifice of eternity" above the recurring renewal of the natural world. But Yeats' Romanticism was always a horse of a different color. Rather than idolizing nature and love, Yeats took up the other great theme of the Romantic movement: self-expression. Since his troubled life spanned a later and more fraught generation than the high Romantic poets like Wordsworth and Keats, his Romanticism was darker and fiercer. Throughout his poetry, Yeats spoke for two selves: one individual and one national. An Irish revolutionary and a passionate lover, his personal life was plagued by the loss and intensity that marks his canon. He was forever searching for the idealized self and the idealized nation, displacing his longings onto the ancient wisdom and beauty of symbolic Byzantium. In spite of his extreme introspection, however, Yeats avoided the trap of self-indulgence that tainted the work of lesser Romantic poets. As we see in "Sailing to Byzantium," Yeats' genius transformed one man's grief and rage at growing old into a masterpiece of art— the eternal song of a golden bird in the ageless and golden city of Byzantium.

Richard Wilbur
1921–2017

Best known for: "Love Calls Us to the Things of This World,"
"A Baroque Wall-Fountain in the Villa Sciarra," "Juggler"

A two-time recipient of the Pulitzer Prize for poetry (1957 and 1989), a recipient of the Robert Frost Medal, the Wallace Stevens Award, the T. S. Eliot Award, two Bollingen prizes, and the Poet Laureate Consultant in Poetry to the Library of Congress in 1987, Richard Wilbur is one of the most decorated poets of the twentieth century despite being primarily a formalist poet in an age of free forms. Given that he was also a well-regarded translator of poetry from multiple languages, a prolific writer of children's verse, and one of the most imitated poets of his time, a case could be made that he was the preeminent American poet since Robert Frost died in 1963. Wilbur's canon—and his approach to his craft—was marked by what Poetry Foundation calls "composed, reflective, and largely optimistic poetry." Of his own work, Wilbur told the *Paris Review,*:

> *I feel that the universe is full of glorious energy, that the energy tends to take pattern and shape, and that the ultimate character of things is comely and good. I am perfectly aware that I say this in the teeth of all sorts of contrary evidence, and that I must be basing it partly on temperament and partly on faith, but that's my attitude.*

His hopefulness and wit became defining characteristics of his work and, by extension, of the poetry of his era. In fact, Donald Hall once wrote that "[T]he typical ghastly poem of the fifties was a Wilbur poem not written by Wilbur, a poem with tired wit and obvious comparisons and nothing to keep the mind or the ear occupied. It wasn't Wilbur's fault, though I expect he will be asked to suffer for it." Years on, it seems, Hall was wrong; Richard Wilbur should apologize for nothing.

{poem}
Love Calls Us to the Things of the World

The eyes open to a cry of pulleys,
And spirited from sleep, the astounded soul
Hangs for a moment bodiless and simple
As false dawn.
     Outside the open window
The morning air is all awash with angels.

 Some are in bed-sheets, some are in blouses,
Some are in smocks: but truly there they are.
Now they are rising together in calm swells
Of halcyon feeling, filling whatever they wear
With the deep joy of their impersonal breathing;

 Now they are flying in place, conveying
The terrible speed of their omnipresence, moving
And staying like white water; and now of a sudden
They swoon down into so rapt a quiet
That nobody seems to be there.
      The soul shrinks

 From all that it is about to remember,
From the punctual rape of every blessèd day,
And cries,
   "Oh, let there be nothing on earth but laundry,

Nothing but rosy hands in the rising steam
And clear dances done in the sight of heaven."

   Yet, as the sun acknowledges
With a warm look the world's hunks and colors,
The soul descends once more in bitter love
To accept the waking body, saying now
In a changed voice as the man yawns and rises,
   "Bring them down from their ruddy gallows;
Let there be clean linen for the backs of thieves;
Let lovers go fresh and sweet to be undone,
And the heaviest nuns walk in a pure floating
Of dark habits,
              keeping their difficult balance."

{reflection}

All That Is Clear and Orderly
by James Matthew Wilson

Among Richard Wilbur's greatest poems stands "Love Calls Us," one of the most admired American poems of the last century. Wilbur's poetry as a whole gives expression to great delight in the finely-wrought existence of the things of this world, so much so that one misguided critic has called him a "hedonist." The poetry itself is also finely wrought, often baroque in its gorgeous intricacies of form and rhyme as well as its playful and extravagant mastery of language. Some of his early critics, also misguided, thought his work a mere aesthete's pleasure in shapeliness and cleverness for its own sake. "Love," with its irregular blank verse meter, may seem less flashy of surface than other Wilbur poems; but it also shows with a directness and clarity just why such criticisms miss the mark. It is a poem that celebrates the way the ordinary and peculiar can be beautiful and, in its beauty, remind us of an extraordinary order—that of the cosmos, governed by soul or spirit, and created from nothing, gratuitously, by God's love. In response to such plentitude, love calls us not chiefly to savor but to bless the things the world.

Sensuous beauty and poetic cleverness are good, this poem suggests, in no small part because they express and so make possible a vision of what is infinitely greater than themselves. Wilbur frequently claimed to have found the phrase that serves as the title of this poem in the pages of Saint Augustine, but was never able to recall the exact place. Whether he remembered correctly or not, the poet and the great theologian were alike in seeing a dynamic interrelation between the material and the spiritual—the external world and the interior ascent of the soul moved by love toward the God who made it. Each draws in his own way on Plato's idea, expressed in the *Phaedrus* and elsewhere, that the soul's primordial vision of intellectual forms in the heavens prepares it to see and understand the visible things of the world. And like Plato and Augustine, Wilbur suggests that only through our vision of the illumination of what is above,can we come to appreciate and love what is here in the world below.

All of this may sound rather elevated for a poem that begins with a familiar, humble image of early-twentieth-century American city life: laundry lines extended between tenement buildings from which hang the light and brilliant washing of the previous day. The poem starts with the startled opening of some city-sleeper's eyes early in the morning; they are our eyes, too, insofar as the poem narrates how any of us might awaken to such a vision and be stirred to dreamy thought by it:

> *The eyes open to a cry of pulleys,*
> *And spirited from sleep, the astounded soul*

> *Hangs for a moment bodiless and simple*
> *As false dawn.*
>   *Outside the open window*
> *The morning air is all awash with angels.*

Our literature contains many visionary poems, the most celebrated of which is Dante's *Divine Comedy*. Dante suddenly "comes to himself" in a dark wood, as if shaken from sleep, and he does not know where he is. So do these eyes open—wakened by the squeak of metal pulleys as someone draws in laundry from the line. They are so sufficiently startled, these eyes, that they seem the organs of the soul, "spirited" and "bodiness," elevated above the physical condition. They open, suspended in "false dawn," meaning wakefulness but before the hour at which we resume the daily grind. In that almost angelic state, they see indeed a whole morning "awash with angels."

As the eyes of the soul come into focus and return, however partially, as it were, to the solidity of the body, the mind realizes where it actually is and observes the literal features of the pieces of hung-out laundry that make them not just to seem but in some sense to be spiritual creatures glimpsed in buoyant, leisured flight:

> *Some are in bed-sheets, some are in blouses,*
> *Some are in smocks: but truly there they are.*
> *Now they are rising together in calm swells*
> *Of halcyon feeling, filling whatever they wear*
> *With the deep joy of their impersonal breathing . . .*

Wilbur offers us not a simile, where one thing seems like another, but a metaphor or a symbol, where the angel really is in the laundry, a spiritual mystery tucked inside a physical form that already reminds us of it. Their floating is akin to jellyfish on the tide, on the "calm swells," such that they are presences whose chief attribute is their transcendent and free way of existing. But the next stanza injects this image with a kind of sublimity:

> *Now they are flying in place, conveying*
> *The terrible speed of their omnipresence, moving*
> *And staying like white water; and now of a sudden*
> *They swoon down into so rapt a quiet*
> *That nobody seems to be there.*

If the first image invites us to a static contemplation of easeful beauty, this one here gives us just a subtle jolt of terror. The sublime, according to the Romantics of two centuries past, was anything in nature that seemed so absolute in its grandeur as to make us feel a thrill at the thought of our own creaturely fragility. When the angel Gabriel appeared to Mary, he had first to say, "Be not afraid," before he could deliver his message. All things of the spirit may strike us with fear because we know that the spirit is absolutely greater than the flesh.

The fear proper to the sublime, however, is complex: It could crush our bodies, yes, but it also promises rapture, ecstasy, to draw us out of our bodily selves so as to discover our own greatness of spirit, which exceeds the tallest of mountains. In Wilbur's poem, this sublime image, for just a second, seems too much for the soul; but, as the lines descend the page, we see that what the soul fears is its return to the body. What the soul immediately desires is to remain in this visionary ecstasy far above the mundane weight of the flesh:

> *The soul shrinks*
>
> *From all that it is about to remember,*
> *From the punctual rape of every blesséd day,*
> *And cries,*
> *   "Oh, let there be nothing on earth but laundry,*
> *Nothing but rosy hands in the rising steam*
> *And clear dances done in the sight of heaven."*

Wilbur has created a neat dualism. The soul and the angelic are identified with transcendence and freedom but also with purity and the ideal. Following Plato, descent into the body and a return to the waking mundane signals a return to a world weighed down, fallen, imperfect, and admixed with grief. The soul thus wishes for an ideal earth of rising sheets and "rising steam," forever dancing like the angels who circle the throne of heaven.

Whether or not Wilbur's title borrows from Augustine, his theme thus far closely echoes the saint's ideas of morning and evening knowledge in *The City of God*. There Augustine says that all creatures have a shadowy, evening knowledge of reality until they see themselves "in the light of God's wisdom" at which moment they attain a truer and more brilliant "morning knowledge." In the poem, the soul's

eyes have a vision of morning knowledge, of the world bathed in the
light of the divine so that matter itself seems but a gown for spirit,
and everything rises up to a state of purity. The soul, however, must
awaken to the actual day in this present world and does so now, but it
is transformed by what it has seen in its rapture:

> *Yet, as the sun acknowledges*
> *With a warm look the world's hunks and colors,*
> *The soul descends once more in bitter love*
> *To accept the waking body, saying now*
> *In a changed voice as the man yawns and rises . . .*

We break in here, mid-sentence, to observe that the soul has returned to its daily home and become a man. The light of heaven now
reveals, not perfect white, but the substantial "hunks" of things whose
colors indicate that they are illuminated by a light above the world
but also that they are the material stuff of this world. This descent is
not the love experienced in transcendent ecstasy but, to the contrary,
one involving certain fallenness into a regime of time and force—the
"punctual rape" of the everyday. And yet, light and love do not hide
themselves in heaven; they come down with us, to the things of the
world, and pour themselves out generously upon it. They say, through
the spoken wish and blessing of the man:

> *"Bring them down from their ruddy gallows;*
> *Let there be clean linen for the backs of thieves;*
> *Let lovers go fresh and sweet to be undone,*

And the heaviest nuns walk in a pure floating
Of dark habits,
> *keeping their difficult balance."*

The day may be fallen and violent, but it is nonetheless "blesséd." The light of heaven is a perfect radiance, but the soul's primordial vision of it becomes, finally, a preparation—to return to the world and to see it in all its materiality, finitude, and imperfection as a true reflection of what transcends it. Having seen beyond what Shelley called the "painted veil" of this world, the soul might be tempted to view things here below with contempt. It does not. No, to the contrary, it brings with it, into the world, light and grace in the form of appreciation and blessing. It sees that the backs of the wicked, which deserve whipping, have also their share of the angelic; lovers, fated to be ruined by the breakup of their romance, participate nonetheless in the divine love; holy women, with the ascetic and so world-denying "habits" and stilted movements, nonetheless "float" in a reminder of the living spirits whose banquet they seek, one day, to join.

In an early interview, Wilbur said that all serious poetry is religious because "it affirms all that is clear and orderly in the world." Heaven delights—so does this world—but they are not two different delectations: The heavenly order bestows itself on the world below, brightening it and lightening it. Meanwhile, the "hunks and colors" of the world below are themselves images and reminders of what the soul may see, between sleeping and waking, of heaven.

William Wordsworth
1770–1850

Best known for: The Prelude, *"I Wandered Lonely as a Cloud,"*
"Ode: Intimations of Immortality"

William Wordsworth was England's premier Romantic poet. Born in 1770 in Cockermouth, Cumbria, England, young William lost his mother when he was eight and his father when he was thirteen, orphaning him and his four siblings. Profoundly influenced by this loss, he wrote his first poems while enrolled at the Hawkshead Grammar School. After graduating in 1791 from Cambridge University, Wordsworth received an inheritance that supported him and his sister Dorothy, with whom he was famously close, and provided him the means to take a walking tour of Europe, a trip that formed his sensibilities toward the solitary contemplation of nature. At the age of twenty-five, Wordsworth developed a working friendship with fellow poet Samuel Taylor Coleridge, with whom he published *Lyrical Ballads* in 1798, launching the English Romantic movement. Speaking for the Romantics, Wordsworth famously described poetry as "the spontaneous overflow of powerful feelings." Romantic poetry is known for effusion of emotion, idealization of nature, and elevation of the status of poet. With the publication of *Lyrical Ballads*, Wordsworth became one of the most influential cultural figures in the Western world. His magnum opus, *The Prelude*, was published posthumously in 1850. Wordsworth became England's poet laureate in 1843, a role he held until his death.

{poem}
The World Is Too Much With Us

The world is too much with us; late and soon,
Getting and spending, we lay waste our powers;—
Little we see in Nature that is ours;
We have given our hearts away, a sordid boon!
This Sea that bares her bosom to the moon;
The winds that will be howling at all hours,
And are up-gathered now like sleeping flowers;
For this, for everything, we are out of tune;
It moves us not. Great God! I'd rather be
A Pagan suckled in a creed outworn;
So might I, standing on this pleasant lea,
Have glimpses that would make me less forlorn;
Have sight of Proteus rising from the sea;
Or hear old Triton blow his wreathèd horn.

{reflection}

Whom Do We Deck in Wreaths?

by Anthony Esolen

I don't know what mischievous devil put it in my head, but I did a little search on the Internet to see what teachers and students are told about this famous sonnet by William Wordsworth. I found some chatter about the grime and drabness of the Industrial Revolution and some standard fare about the form of the poem (a Petrarchan sonnet), the meter (iambic pentameter), and personification. Mostly it was irrelevant, imprecise, or wrong. Don't go to such places, dear reader.

"The world is too much with us," says the poet. Obviously he doesn't mean the world of moon and seas and meadows. Then what? "The sorrow of the world worketh death," says Saint Paul to the church at Corinth, warning them against desires to which the world is bound (2 Cor. 7:10 [KJV]). "Love not the world," says Saint John, "neither the things that are in the world … the lust of the flesh, and the lust of the eyes, and the pride of life, is not of the Father, but is of the world" (1 John 2:15–16 [KJV]). Our avarice and ambition, our "getting and spending," our having the world too much with us, is vanity: "Ye that say, To day or to morrow we will go to such a city, and continue there a year, and buy and sell, and get gain: Whereas ye know not what shall be on the morrow," for death is the end of worldly things (Jas. 4:13–14 {KJV}).

A life of getting and spending is no more meaningful than eating and evacuating. We need not wait for the punishment. The worldliness punishes itself: "We lay waste our powers," says the poet—spiritual and intellectual powers, devastated as by continual war. "For what shall it profit a man," says Jesus, "if he shall gain the whole world, and lose his own soul?" (Mark 8:36 [KJV]). "We have given our hearts away, a sordid boon!" cries the poet, with breathless exasperation—"we have" and "given" are pronounced each as a single syllable. What have we gained with our restless worldliness? We lose our hearts, and we lose the world—not the world of getting and spending but the mysterious and beautiful creation around us.

That world is the focus of attention for the rest of the poem. The poet is gazing upon "[t]his Sea that bares her bosom to the moon," a lovely and evocative line as if the now calm and swelling sea were a woman laying herself bare to her lover, the moon, and thus do the tides come in. He hears the quiet of winds "that will be howling at all hours," meaning not that they do so, but that they want to, and now they are all gathered up "like sleeping flowers," and we can see the shut petals in the calm of evening. "For this, for everything, we are out of tune," he says, and at this point in most sonnets, the sentence would end the line, and the line would end the octet, the opening eight lines set apart from the final six. But Wordsworth does better here. He cracks his own form, delaying the sentence's end till the broken first half of line nine: "It moves us not." It is as if a doctor were to look up from a body and say, simply and bluntly, "He is dead." We are a musical instrument whose strings have gone slack, and the winds of beauty sweep across us without effect. Such is the dullness of the "world."

Here Wordsworth cries out to rouse us from our dead sleep: "Great God!" That is no mere exclamation. He wants to remind us of God and the world he has made. He does not wish he were a pagan. He says he would prefer to be a pagan "suckled in a creed outworn," taking it in with his mother's milk rather than be a worldly man of his time, getting and spending with a soul laid waste. Anything would be better than that exhaustion! But he lays a condition on his wish. It would be worth it to be that pagan, with all his old-fashioned beliefs, "So might I, standing on this pleasant lea,/Have glimpses that would make me less forlorn." We must get the grammar correct here. He means that he would sooner be a pagan provided that he might have those glimpses. The force is ironic. Neither Wordsworth nor his readers took seriously any resumption of Greek paganism. It was impossible after the revelation of Christ. But if you had to be something, you would be better off with a real human heart so that you could have a real human experience of the natural world.

That experience, to come from a full heart and not one that has been rendered a wasteland by the modern war of avarice and ambition, must be a religious one. Wordsworth does not use Proteus, the shape-changing god of the deeps of the sea, and Triton, his horn-winding herald, as mere poetic personifications. Nor does he intend that we worship them as gods. There is no returning to that dawn of the pagan myth. We really should hear and feel the divine at work within these natural things. God has made them, and God dwells within them; He works in them and through them. The modern reduction that they are only soil, water, or movements of air caused by variations in pressure—a variety of flora taking nitrates from the earth and carbon dioxide from the air—is a swindle. We get and spend, and we lose the soul. We immerse ourselves in the world, and we can no longer see things as they are. We can see only this or that measurable or utilitarian feature: not the rich earth, not the dangerous sea, not the shut flowers. "We murder to dissect," says Wordsworth in another well-known poem.

One last suggestion: Triton's horn is "wreathéd," and that word "too" is not just meant to be picturesque or poetical. We are meant to see the strange lush greens of the ocean all wound about that horn as the herald has risen up from a world that is here for us to see a little of but is in itself too wonderfully deep to fathom. And whom do we deck in wreaths? Those blest in the arts, the laureates, and the victors in beauty. Who would not rather listen to the poet than to the automatic bids of men on a stock exchange?

Acknowledgements

My sincere thanks to each of the writers who contributed to this book. They are poets, scholars, teachers, and friends, and this book is what it is because of them. Thanks to my wife, Bethany, who has a sense for what works (and whose longsuffering provided the space to work on this project single-mindedly when necessary); to Kirstie Ruffatto whose original illustrations of the poets belong on walls not just tucked away inside these pages; to Graeme Pitman for his grand cover design, the skill neither of us knew he had when we met years ago; to Heidi White, who helped with key details along the way; and to Kristen Rudd, whose careful and critical eye kept this book from being an embarrassment.

Thanks to the community of the Close Reads podcast network, especially those who tune in to *The Daily Poem*. Your feedback pushed this project along, but your reverence for the poems themselves was the impetus for its creation. What a joyful, thoughtful group of people you are. Happy reading.

Thanks to my parents who taught me to love beautiful words.

Contributors

Emily Andrews is an Associate Director at CenterForLit and an Associate Editor for *FORMA Journal*. She received a degree in History and English Literature from Hillsdale College where she met her husband, Ian. Now they live in Spokane, Washington where they write, teach, podcast, and unsuccessfully battle a book-collecting addiction.

Ian Andrews is an Associate Director at CenterForLit. He is a graduate of Hillsdale College where he received a degree in English Literature and met his wife, Emily. The Andrews live in Spokane, Washington, where they spend their days teaching, writing, podcasting, and developing teacher resources in literature. Their evenings are spent pursuing a love of good food, good wine, and well-told stories in every medium.

Jeffrey Bilbro is an Associate Professor of English at Spring Arbor University as well as the Editor-in-Chief for Front Porch Republic. His books include *Virtues of Renewal: Wendell Berry's Sustainable Forms* and *Wendell Berry and Higher Education: Cultivating Virtues of Place* (written with Jack Baker).

Matthew Bianco is the Vice President of Training for the CiRCE Institute where he also serves as a head mentor in the CiRCE Apprenticeship program. A homeschooling father of three, he has graduated all of his children, the eldest of whom graduated from St. John's College in Annapolis, Maryland. His middle child graduated Belmont Abbey College in Charlotte, North Carolina, where his youngest still attends. He is married to his altogether lovely high-school sweetheart, Patricia. He is the author of *Letters to*

My Sons: A Humane Vision for Human Relationships.

Anthony Esolen is a writer, social commentator, translator of classical poetry, and Writer-in-Residence at Magdalen College of the Liberal Arts. He
taught at Furman University and Providence College before transferring to
the Thomas More College of Liberal Arts in 2017 and Magdalen in 2019.
Esolen has translated into English Dante's *Divine Comedy*, Lucretius' *On
the Nature of Things*, and Torquato Tasso's *Jerusalem Delivered*. In addition to
multiple books, he is the author of numerous articles in such publications as
The Modern Age, *The Catholic World Report*, *The Claremont Review of Books*,
The Public Discourse, *First Things*, *Crisis Magazine*, and *Touchstone*, for which
he serves as a senior editor.

A. M. Juster is the author of ten books of original and translated poetry, including *Wonder and Wrath* (Paul Dry Books 2020). He has won the Howard
Nemerov Sonnet Award three times, the Richard Wilbur Award for his first
book of original poetry, the Barnstone Translation Prize, and the Alzhei-
mer's Association's Humanitarian of the Year Award. His work has appeared
in *Poetry*, *Paris Review*, *Hudson Review*, *Rattle*, and many other journals.

Maurice Manning has published seven collections of poetry, most recently
Railsplitter. His fourth book, *The Common Man*, was a finalist for the Pulitzer Prize. A former Guggenheim fellow, Manning lives with his family on
a small farm in Kentucky. He is professor of English and the writer-in-residence at Transylvania University, and he also teaches in the MFA Program
for Writers at Warren Wilson College.

Since graduating from The University of Maryland MFA program in 2001 (and Johns Hopkins in 1991), **Christine Perrin** has taught poetry at Johns Hopkins University, Messiah College, and Gordon College's Orvieto Program. She directs the writing program at Messiah College. She is a two-time recipient of the Pennsylvania Arts Council Artists Fellowship. She is the poetry editor of *FORMA Journal*. Her own work appears in various journals including *The New England Review, The Cresset, Image, TriQuarterly, Blackbird,* and *Christianity and Literature. Bright Mirror* is her first book of poetry. She is married to Christopher Perrin, and they live in Pennsylvania.

Brian Phillips is the pastor of Holy Trinity Reformed Church (Concord, NC), an adjunct faculty member at Belmont Abbey College, and a teacher-writer-consultant for the CiRCE Institute. After turning forty, he decided to pursue a childhood dream and also became an EMT. He is the author/editor of several books, including *Sunday Mornings: An Introduction to Biblical Worship* and *Tales of Wonder* (Volumes I & II). He and his wife Shannon have two sons, two daughters, and a dog named Ajax the Great.

Sally Thomas was born in 1964 in Memphis, Tennessee, and was educated at Vanderbilt University, the University of Memphis, and the University of Utah. She is the author of two poetry chapbooks, *Fallen Water* (2015) and *Richeldis of Walsingham* (2016), both from Finishing Line Press and of a poetry collection, *Motherland,* a finalist for the 2018 Able Muse Book Award available from Able Muse Press. Over the last two decades, her poetry, fiction, and essays have appeared in *Dappled Things, First Things, Forma, Local Culture, Mezzo Cammin, North American Anglican, Plough Quarterly, Presence, Relief, Southern Poetry Review*, the *New Yorker*, and the *Windhover*. She lives with her family in the Western Piedmont of North Carolina.

Heidi White, M.A., teaches humanities at St. Hild School in Colorado Springs. She is the Managing Editor at *FORMA Journal*, the host of the *FORMA Podcast,* and a featured contributor at the Close Reads Podcast Network and the *Redeemed Imagination* podcast. A frequent lecturer and conference speaker on literature, education, and the Christian Imagination, Heidi equips people to read and teach literature, Great Books, and the Classics. Heidi serves on the CLT Academic Advisory Board. She has published essays, book reviews, and poetry at the CiRCE Institute, *FORMA Journal*, the Anselm Society, enCourage, Story Warren, and more. She lives, writes, and teaches in Black Forest, Colorado.

James Matthew Wilson is the author of nine books, including *The River of the Immaculate Conception, The Hanging God,* and *The Vision of the Soul: Truth, Goodness, and Beauty in the Western Tradition.* A poet, critic, and scholar of philosophical-theology and literature, he was the 2017 recipient of the Hiett Prize from the Dallas Institute of Humanities and Culture. Wilson serves as poetry editor of Modern Age magazine, director of the Colosseum Institute, series editor of Colosseum Books, and is associate professor of Humanities and Augustinian Traditions at Villanova University.

Jessica Hooten Wilson is an associate professor of humanities at John Brown University. She is the author of three books, including the 2018 *Christianity Today* book of the year in arts and culture, *Giving the Devil His Due.* She is the 2019 winner of the Hiett Prize in the Humanities from the Dallas Institute of Humanities and Culture.

Credits

About the Editor

David Kern is the host of *The Daily Poem* and *Close Reads* podcasts, the editor-in-chief of *FORMA Journal*, and the Vice President of Integrated Resources for the CiRCE Institute. He and his family live in North Carolina.